MOVE OVER JUDAS

HOW MY FAITHLESS BETRAYAL COLLIDED WITH

THE LOVE AND FORGIVENESS OF JESUS CHRIST

TREVER ROOK

A MEMOIR

DEDICATION

To the ones I harmed

CONTENTS

MOVE OVER JUDAS

ACKNOWLEDGMENTS

Several people played a part in getting this book written. Along with the many coffee places and coffees, I'd like to thank my son Trevin Rook for his loving support and understanding during the times I had to write.

I owe thanks to my friends Trish and Steve Todd for looking over rough ideas and listening to me brainstorm in many directions.

Grateful thanks to Jamie Brown for pounding on the widow.

Special thanks to my editor Kelly Madigan for her wisdom, honesty, and friendship.

Thanks to my mother Shirley Clark, for loving me when I really didn't deserve it.

And of course, a big thank you to that Jesus guy for keeping his hand on my shoulder at all times even when I tried so hard to pull away.

.

FORWARD

After reading the first draft of my good friend Trever's soul-baring story, my palms felt a little sweaty. "Does he really want his son to read this? And his mom? What about the people in his church?"

So I called him up and asked why he was writing it. Who did he hope would read it? Why did he want them to read it?

He said he hoped that by reading his story people would get what God's grace is all about. That if they see how God did not give up on someone like him, maybe they'll believe that God hasn't given up on them either. And he's right. This is a story about grace. Despite many years of pain and poor choices, God continued to hang around.

Some of you will find you have a lot in common with Trever, especially when it comes to the junk you've been through. Or your story may be very different. Either way, we all need grace.

Trever tells his story because he believes that, like the Apostle Paul who called himself the worst of sinners (1 Timothy 1:16), he's an example of Jesus' tremendous patience and mercy.

This book also serves as a reminder that many of us have a dark closet of insecurity we keep safely hidden from view. In Trever's case, it was masked by his gift for making people laugh. But he learned that healing could not be found by hiding. God has another way.

The Good News is that Jesus takes our broken stories and rewrites them. This book is a testimony to his grace.

Steve Todd
Pastor, Faith Westwood United Methodist Church
Omaha, Nebraska

PREFACE

While reading the rough drafts, my editor asked if I was sure I wanted things in this book to be known. "You really weren't a nice guy in this." She warned.

To say I wasn't a nice guy is quite an understatement. In my opinion, I was a monster.

The apostle Paul called himself the greatest sinner of all time. I imagine one's opinion as to the degree of sinfulness is relative to their personal beliefs. This book is based on my personal opinions and beliefs and is in no way aimed at anyone's behavior or choices but my own.

The focus of this book is that of my wrong doings and how I harmed and betrayed those around me. It's written from my personal memories of my life. There may be dates I got wrong or things I have left out, but I assure you, it is an honest look into my life.

I do want to give a few warnings before you begin reading. By the title, you will know this is not a book about someone who did good things. It is filled with terrible choices and ugly behavior. In some places there is language and subjects for mature audiences. This is an honest book of a sinner and the content and language are part of that honesty.

As an individual, this book is a confessional and an apology. As a Pastor, this book is testimony that even the best of sinners can be rescued.

Most importantly, this book is about forgiveness, love and grace.

MOVE OVER JUDAS

Then Judas, which had betrayed him, when he saw that he was condemned, repented himself, and brought again the thirty pieces of silver to the chief priests and elders, saying, I have sinned in that I have betrayed the innocent blood. And they said, what is that to us? See thou to that. And he cast down the pieces of silver in the temple, and departed, and went and hanged himself.

~Matthew 27:3-5(KJV)

MOVE OVER JUDAS

ONE

"Unlock the door, you idiot!" Jamie yelled as he struggled to get into the passenger's side of my car.

I don't know where he came from, but he scared me so much the pills fell out of my hand and onto the floor mat. It seems the hardest thing about a suicide attempt is trying to find some peace and quiet in which to do it. At this point I didn't know what to do next. Do I unlock the door for Jamie or do I reach down and pick up the pills? I gathered the first decision I made was incorrect, because as I reached for the pills Jamie begin to actually physically shake the car door.

"I said unlock the car door!" He yelled again as he continued to try to force the door open.

"I really don't like your tone!" I yelled back.

I really didn't. I mean, here I was at my wit's end trying to commit suicide, and I've got this guy shaking my car and being pretty darn rude to me.

"Unlock the door or I'll break the window!" He yelled back, obviously not caring what I felt at the time.

I sighed dramatically and hit the door unlock

button, but it didn't take because Jamie was wiggling the car door at the time.

"Unlock it!" He yelled.

"I did!"

"No, you didn't!"

"Stop wiggling the handle!"

"Unlock it!"

"I'm trying!"

This back and forth seemed to go on three or four more times until Jamie finally calmed down enough to stop wiggling the car door so I could successfully unlock it. Then it was like a herd of elephants in the form of one man as he dove between my legs to pick up the pills. In my confused state, I protected my crotch, not knowing exactly what he was going for.

"Trever, what do you think you're doing?" He asked, after picking up the pills.

"Protecting my crotch." I said nervously.

Jamie took full advantage of that and hit me in the arm.

"Killing yourself is the most selfish thing you have ever done." He yelled.

"I obviously haven't killed myself." I said, with a tone that may have been interpreted as sarcasm.

Jamie hit me in the arm again. I guess he interpreted it correctly.

"Ouch!" I yelled, "I chose the pills to *avoid* pain!"

Jamie hit me in the arm again.

"Would you stop hitting me?" I asked. "I'm pretty sure punching someone isn't in the handbook of suicide prevention."

"Don't give me any of that crap!" Jamie yelled. It was becoming obvious to me Jamie had never read any kind of handbook on suicide prevention.

"You of all people should know this will pass." He said.

Jamie knew much of my history. We had been friends for a while and worked together at the church for many years. Well, he worked. I volunteered. He was the music director and I was kind of the resident comedian. I did funny characters and videos to add elements to the sermons. They were pretty popular.

I always told people I added the comedy elements because I had a passion to make church a bit more approachable to newcomers. And while that part was true, I admit I also liked the attention. So much so I think church became more about me than about Who I was there to worship. I began to pay less and less attention to the messages and focused more on how many laughs I was getting. But it was more than just the attention. For me, entertaining was a need.

Jamie hit me in the arm again.

"Did you hear what I said?"

"Yes! I answered, "And for future reference, the next time you have a question, you don't have to hit me!"

"Did you take any pills before I got to the car?" He asked.

Finally, I thought, a question that could have come from a handbook.

"What if I did?" I asked sarcastically, "Are you going to hit me again?"

I guess I asked for it that time. He hit me again.

"Did you take any pills?" he asked.

"No!"

"You've been through this before and you'll get through it again."

When Jamie used the phrase, "through this before;" my insides shriveled into nothing. For the first time in the conversation, I found myself unable to give a sarcastic reply.

Real tears began to roll down my face. I began to cry harder than I had in many years. I tried my best to hold them back but couldn't. I was suddenly so overtaken by emotion I couldn't speak. Jamie just sat there and watched as I crumbled into a ball. Finally, I was able to get out just a few words.

"I can't take any more pain," I cried.

"I know." He replied. "I doubt I could deal with the pain you've gone through in your life."

Those weren't really the magic words of wisdom I was hoping for. By this time I actually considered buying a book on suicide prevention and just reading it to him.

However in the state of mind I was in, I could not agree with Jamie more. My pain had seemed to hit its limit. My third wife had just left me and I was packing up and moving my son and me to yet another apartment. I had failed as a husband, I had failed as a father, and I had betrayed God.

I guess feeling sorry for yourself is a requirement for a suicidal state of mind. However, there were deeper feelings than those just lying on the surface.

But what exactly led me to this moment? Why was I in a car with a handful of pills and a caring friend punching me repeatedly? What was the source of all this pain I could no longer take? What were the events and situations that lead me to a suicide attempt?

At that moment I began to look back at my life, beginning with my earliest memory.

TWO

I'm sitting in my crib with my twin brother. We're not identical twins as I learn from hearing us described by family and friends, "Todd is the cute one with the biggest blue eyes, and Trever is the fat one with curly hair."

My brother was always described with adjectives like 'cute, adorable, quiet, neat,' while I got monikers like 'the bigger one, hollow leg, and oh my God he's huge!'

Just a side note here; if you are ever visiting someone who has a baby, never say things like "Oh my God, he's huge!" even if the kid weighs more than the car you drove there. It's just not a good thing to say.

I had those kinds of labels on me from the day I was born. My brother and I made quite an impact on that day, being that we were one of the heaviest set of twins to be born that year in Lincoln, Nebraska. Today, there are probably plenty of twins coming in at 8 ½ and 10 pounds, but I guess it was a big deal in 1969. We were the talk of the town according to my mother, but I'm guessing it was more like we were the talk of the hospital.

I apparently stole most of that talk, being the one that weighed ten pounds. My extra 1 ½ pounds would forever protect my brother from ever being regarded as big.

My early eating habits did not help to diffuse this new found reputation either. My mom said I was eating solid food before I even left the hospital. This too caused a bit of a stir among nurses, doctors and other hospital spectators. I guess when you enter the world like that, people are bound to typecast you as an over-eater.

Being known as a good eater isn't exactly terrible when one is raised in the Midwest. Growing up in small-town Nebraska, we were taught to be respectful of agriculture and the consumption of corn and cows were two of our biggest exports.

Actually I don't remember ever being on a farm. We lived in a town called Waverly that was surrounded by farmland but I always thought I was raised in a city. The only reminder of the farms was an occasional whiff of livestock, strong enough to make one scared to go outside, open a window, or even inhale. That could make it difficult to eat the exports but we didn't suffer much. My dad worked at a meat-packing plant and my mother was a stay-at-home mom.

Dad's job was in Lincoln and he would drive about 20 minutes there and back each day to go to work. Aside from the local school teachers, no one worked in Waverly. There just weren't any jobs. While it seemed like a city to me growing up, the town was perhaps a much closer fit to Mayberry from *The Andy Griffith Show.*

When the shows weren't on, I would usually be playing with my brother Todd outside. Some of the neighborhood kids would join us in the back yard for a game of cops and robbers or tag. Actually looking back, I think both games were the same thing.

My brother and I were very close when we were young. We shared a room together for the first few years of our lives and slept in bunk beds. I was scared of the dark and my brother and I would often take our minds off our fears by reciting Ernie and Bert routines we saw on *Sesame Street* that day, trading off who played who. We would get to laughing so hard my parents would yell at us from the living room to go to sleep. If it got too out-of-hand my father would come in. That was never a cure for being scared of the dark.

Growing up, I think I feared my father more than anything. My dad wasn't a tall man, standing at only about 5' 7", but he was a big man. Lugging beef for so many years at the packing house gave him a physique resembling a gorilla. His arms were the size of most dads' legs. He was, beyond a doubt, the toughest man in town and everyone knew it. There was always kind of a frightened respect from the other fathers. They would often come over to our house and hang out on the front porch.

Most people can tell it's summer by the way the wind feels and by the way the trees look. I could tell because that's when our front porch was filled with fat guys in cut-off shorts that were way too short. (It was the seventies) My dad would laugh and joke around with all the other fathers as my mom would yuck it up with the wives.

I can still smell the burps coming from all these overweight parents as they tried their best to look sophisticated but no one looks sophisticated when they are burping up Schlitz. That may truly be the only thing that makes the livestock smell better by comparison.

At first the drunken get-togethers didn't seem that bad. The parents would laugh and gab while we would play with the neighborhood kids and since the parents were two shades to the wind, it never mattered how long we stayed out at night. Sometimes it would be past midnight and you could still see the parents stewing it up while a bunch of little kids play under a dim street light in front of the house. But after a while the summer porch nights began to take on a darker side where testosterone and alcohol proved to be a bad mix.

On our fifth or sixth birthday, my parents bought my brother and me a pair of boxing gloves. I'm not sure, but I think it was at first, an effort to encourage some exercise and maybe get chubby Trever to lose some weight. We would run outside and box each other while my parents filmed it on the home movie camera. Neither one of us knew what we were doing nor am I sure any real punches were thrown. It was more like two kids waving their arms frantically and just colliding into each other until one got knocked to the ground. My weight became an advantage because I could shift it and basically bowl over my brother like I was a sumo wrestler.

In our childlike innocence we would bring the gloves along when we played with the neighborhood kids, taking turns colliding into each other and I would use my chubbiness to wave my arms and push kids over every time. That's what happened on one of the summer porch nights but the giggling between kids turned into tears.

The drunken parents got the idea to actually put kids against each other for their entertainment. They would have us fight each other and place bets on the winners, which were determined by which child could make the other cry. Suddenly my super chub powers were no longer used for good and I was quickly crowned champ after making my friends cry. The parents even made me fight my older sister after the neighborhood kids eventually refused to put on the gloves.

THREE

My parents were a product of mid-America in the 50's and 60's. In those times, everyone drank and smoked. You were given funny looks if you didn't. And in the heartland, men were tough brutes that enjoyed beer, Marlboro reds, and football.

I think every dad wanted to be James Bond, but most in my neighborhood fell short and were more like Ralph Kramden from *The Honeymooners*. That was my dad. On his good days he was more like Fred Flintstone. He was funny and childlike and enjoyed a good prank now and then.

One time at the dinner table I was reaching for the salt and my dad slammed his hand down on the table just as the salt was passing my milk. I jumped a mile and the salt fell right into my glass. My dad laughed so hard he almost fell out of his chair. The next day at dinner he asked me to pass him the salt and waited until, again, it was right over my glass and yelled "Trever don't drop the salt!" Naturally I jumped yet again and the salt was once more in the glass of milk.

Dad was so proud and laughed all night. He even bragged to his friends he was able to scare me and twice make the salt drop into the glass. To this day passing salt makes me flinch and I cannot drink milk.

As a child I did not know my dad was an alcoholic, nor did I even know what alcoholism was at that age. Like I said, everyone drank. But while the neighbors saw the happy drunk, we kids saw something that scared the hell out of us.

My dad would often become quite temperamental behind closed doors and that would too often lead to physical abuse. A time I remember in particular involved the boxing gloves. I was outside colliding into my friend with the gloves. We were having a good time because no one was placing bets. I had to go to the restroom. I told my friend I would be right back but when I came inside my dad was standing at the front window with a beer in his hand.

"You chickened out of that fight didn't you." he said with burning red eyes.

And before I could say anything, he had me by the back of the neck and was moving me down the hallway, slamming my face into each side of the wall until we got to my bedroom.

"Don't come out until you're ready to be a man." he yelled as he literally threw me in and slammed the door behind me.

I stayed there the rest of the night, and the next day my dad was back to normal.

I'm not sure my dad knew what to think of me. I was kind of an alien to him. While he enjoyed his beer and sports and other manly things like that, I was playing with puppets and acting out Sesame Street bits.

I wrote my first play when I was in second grade. It was a comedy about a king and princes that were kidnapped. I performed it at my school and even got in the local paper as a "Budding Playwright."

While this made me proud it seemed to embarrass my parents. Being in a small town in the seventies, a parent would be proud if their son had scored the winning touchdown or even if they kicked the crap out of some other parent's son, but it was a bit unnerving to have their puppeteer playwright in the paper for all to see. It was something we just didn't talk about.

Football actually came easy to me when I was a kid. I was a good tackler and even a better runner. I would zig and zag and score nearly every time I had the ball. Looking back, that must have killed my parents. Here they had a possible Tony Dorset who preferred to play with Ernie and Bert.

While my dad was obvious about his disappointment in me, my mother seemed to try a more positive approach. She would buy me and my brother football uniforms and act like it was the best thing in the world.

The one person I had in my corner growing up was my dad's mom, Grandma Grace.

I would spend the night at my grandma and grandpa's house often and performed puppet shows while grandma cheered. She would sit on the end of the couch and I would sit on the floor in front of her and talk to her through the puppets. She would ask the puppets questions and we would just be silly all day long.

In the evening grandpa would build a fort out of the couch cushions and I would fall asleep while they watched TV and in the morning I'd wake to the smell of bacon and eggs and coffee.

Grandpa worked at an animal feed store selling pet and bird food. After breakfast we would go out and fill about five bird feeders and then watch from the bay window as the cardinals, blue jays, and squirrels fought over dibs. Afterwards my Grandpa would disappear into the garage.

His hobby was wood working and he would spend hours putting boards through a jigsaw and pulling out various items for his grand kids. My brother and I had these long dump truck toy boxes he made us and a coat hanger in the shape of a giraffe. It was nice but a big wooden giraffe with coats on it can look pretty scary at night to a kid with a good imagination.

The rest of the day at grandmas would be spent doing puppet shows and playing. She would tell me I was so creative and I was sure to be famous someday.

The only time we would take a break was for Grandma's 'bath time.' She would spend about an hour in there while I watched more TV. It wasn't until I was an adult I learned Grandma would use the time to sneak cigarettes. She may have also needed a bit of a break. I'm sure all day long puppet shows can get tiresome even for the most encouraging of people.

Toward the end of the day, they would drive me through McDonald's and then return me home where the creativity would go back into hiding and I would play again in my room alone.

Some of the loneliness was healed one evening when my dad came home in one of his sober good moods. He walked inside and called us into the kitchen. Then out of his coat, he pulled a puppy. It was a schnoodle; half schnauzer half poodle.

She was all black except for a small white patch on her chest and mouth. She was so tiny and happy. All three of us kids just yelped with excitement and my dad and mom were truly gleaming with joy.

We all sat on the kitchen floor as the new family member sniffed us all over. Dad said we should all try to think of a name and after several misses, I had what I thought was a hit. Of course my only references were television and I pulled from the classic Flintstones when I yelled out "Bam Bam!"

"You can't name the dog Bam Bam," said my brother Todd, "it's a girl dog."

Before I could come up with a rebuttal my sister proclaimed "Pebbles!"

And the family cheered with overwhelming approval. Even today when our dog is mentioned, my sister gets the credit for naming her, but I know there would not have been a Pebbles had I not first said Bam Bam. Oh well. She may have gotten the name, but I got the dog.

Pebbles took to me immediately. We played together, stole food together and even talked together.

Pebbles shared my room at night and would hide food in my blankets. One time while crawling into bed, I pulled back the covers and found a half eaten cupcake smashed between the sheets. I never told on her and she ate the rest of it that night.

After a while my parents had trouble telling us apart. They would often get our names mixed around. It was funny around the house but when my mom went outside to yell "Come here Trever," in her babiest of voices it became a bit embarrassing.

FOUR

While Pebbles remained my greatest friend I did find a human to pal around with. His name was Paul and we first met in grade school. He was chubby like me and dare I say, even a bit more so.

I don't remember how we met or how the friendship began but I do remember Paul having the same love for imagination as I did. We played together all the time, doing puppet shows and pretending to be the Superfriends. We both loved Superman and would "fly" all around Paul's back yard.

Landing became an issue when Paul climbed up onto his dad's storage shed and jumped off. It was the first time I saw Superman fall face down and cry after a landing. And to show just how smart we were, I was about to try it myself even after seeing Paul's dive, but his mother made me get down.

After a while we used our creative skills to invent our own superheroes. I found a shirt with the number 14 on it so I became captain 14. Paul was my sidekick captain 9. (I bet you can't tell what he had on his shirt.) We would don our shirts, and with our father's handkerchiefs tied over our faces, impress the kids that were too young to be in school or know any better.

I think Paul's family was the first real look I had into a religious family. They were Mormons and went to church every week and prayed before every meal. My family attempted to go to the Methodist church down the street but the excitement over church just never seemed to stick.

My only memory of Sunday school is lying to the teachers in order to get more Kool-Aid. We were only allowed two Dixie cups full of the watered down stuff but I would play one teacher against the other and say I never got the second cup. I think three cups equaled the right amount of sugar for one anyway.

Whatever they were teaching in that church my family just didn't seem to be interested in. God remained a distant mystery and from an early age I felt maybe He was more available for others. Good people like Paul's family.

Paul's dad wasn't tough or scary like my dad. He may have been the first dad I ever saw that wasn't like the ones on my street. Staying at Paul's was definitely better than staying at my house and sometimes I would wish that somehow Paul and I could become brothers.

As scary as my dad was, there were times when he did seem better than other dads. I remember Saturday mornings very fondly. Like any child in the seventies, Saturday mornings were spent in front of the television watching cartoons. *Superfriends, Flintstones*, and of course, *Looney Tunes*.

My dad loved cartoons. Like one of the kids, he would join us every Saturday with a box of Cheerios. We ate our cereal in bowls but dad always ate his by the handful right out of the box while doing his best impressions of Yosemite Sam and Foghorn Leghorn.

In addition to cartoons, my dad gets credit for my love of classic comedy. No matter what time of day or night, he would call us kids into the living room if there was anything on with Abbott and Costello or Laurel and Hardy or the Three Stooges.

When I was about 8 years old, my grandpa made me a puppet stage in his wood shop. It was a white table top stage and I was beyond thrilled when I got it. For months it sat in my room on a TV tray where I put on shows for Pebbles. When I wasn't using it for a stage, it was the justice league for my super hero figures. One Saturday afternoon I was performing for Pebbles when my dad came into the room.

"Your stage is missing something." he said. "Come with me."

With that, he grabbed my stage off the TV tray. I followed him to the garage and I watched as he sat it on top of his work bench.

Oh, the mighty bench. This is where my dad fixed everything from kitchen crock-pots to cars. But on that day it had been cleaned off and held my precious puppet stage.

I had no idea what dad was going to do to it and was a bit scared to be honest. I knew his feelings about my puppets.

"You need a name for your act." He said while actually smiling.

"A what?" I said with my jaw to the floor.

"Every performing act has a name." he said "Like Jim Henson has *The Muppets*."

I was speechless. I didn't even think he knew who Jim Henson was.

He sat there and stared at my puppet stage thinking while I stared at him with utter shock.

"What about Follies?" He asked, "Back in the vaudeville days people would use the name follies, like Ziegfeld Follies. We could call your act The Trever Rook Follies."

The very sound of that made my fallen jaw turn into a smile. And then I saw the same meticulous genius my dad used when fixing a microwave being used to stencil in the name "Trever Rook Follies" onto my puppet stage; one letter at a time. Measuring the spaces and making sure to keep all letters straight. I think it took him nearly two hours to make the perfect title to my puppet act.

While he worked on it we talked for the first and only time about my puppets.

FIVE

Like any alcoholic, dad's drinking continued to get worse and so did the fighting. He never once laid a hand on my mom, but continued to hit us kids more and more.

He seemed to take out most of his aggression on my brother. I think by the time we were about eight or nine, my dad kind of gave up on me. He knew I wasn't going to be the tough kid he wanted and in a way, his confidence in my brother Todd to carry on the tougher image caused him to focus more negatively on him. While he continued to hit us all, he would often end his attacks with Todd, giving him the brunt of it all. One time he hit him so hard there were actual hand prints on his face.

I can't say I remember my parents ever really getting along. I'm sure at one time they truly loved each other, but growing up, all I saw was hatred. It never mattered what they were talking about or what we were doing, the fights would begin with a comment, then turn to hollering and screaming, and end with my dad punching some metal lockers we had downstairs. He'd hit them so hard it sounded like thunder throughout the house. While he did that my mother would yell at no one in particular about how stupid my dad was.

We kids knew to stay out of the way when things hit the fan. Often times my sister Staci would gather my brother and I into her room and we would wait things out. She seemed to know when it was safe to come back out.

Staci was a good older sister to have. She was two years older and often tried to protect my brother and me from bullies and from the fights of my parents although she did often act a bit like the bully herself.

One time I remember she told me the characters on Sesame Street could hear me and would talk back to me if they liked me. My mom had to take us to the store and I pleaded with Ernie and Bert to please wait until I got back to continue the show but they would not answer me and just kept going.

"I guess they just don't like you." my sister said.

The physical violence and constant fighting did have an obvious effect on us kids. We started to fight with each other more and our verbal arguments would nearly always lead to pretty brutal fights. Apart from the time my sister threw me off a chair and broke my thumb, I was the actual bully of the family.

I would beat up on my brother a lot. We were twins but he was smaller than I and it was easy to overpower him. Many times the fights would take place in front of his friends and he would be humiliated.

On one occasion, I was beating him up in the living room while his friends watched until he ran to the room crying. I sat in the chair like a tough guy until Todd came out of the room with a crazy look in his eyes and a baseball bat in his hand.

He charged at me and swung for my head but I crunched down and blocked it with my leg. This time I went running to my room crying and also got a little taste of how it felt to be beaten. Soon after, my brother would become the one I feared instead of him fearing me.

On a summer night when I was about nine, my parents went out for the evening and left us with a babysitter. He was an older brother of a friend of Todd's that lived down the street. By this time the bat incident was now legend and my brother and sister, along with their friends had begun making fun of my love for puppets and things. I was definitely no longer the tough guy. That part of my life was very short-lived.

There were about ten kids playing in our front yard at the time. I was inside with Pebbles for the most part, but eventually came outside to see what the other kids were doing.

The babysitter had everyone in a huddle and then called me over. As soon as I got there I was tackled by every kid as they dog-piled on top of me, smashing my face into the ground. I could not breathe and was in a total panic.

This was the start of some terrifying claustrophobia that would be used to bully me for years. After learning I would panic every time, the kids would often attack me and lock me in a closet or gang pile on top of me. The panic I felt would give me the strength to throw kids off of me no matter how many were on.

My tearful escapes became entertainment for my siblings and their friends and they would try new ways to trap me. I recall one time being tied to a basketball pole while covered head to toe with an old army tent. They used ropes and I was wrapped like a mummy. By the time I freed myself I was exhausted from panic and from crying my eyes out.

Eventually the constant arguing took a toll and my parents filed for divorce. I think I was about 9 at the time. At first my mom moved out and into an apartment alone and I remember crying myself to sleep every night. Sometimes my dad would come in and try to get me to stop. He wasn't mean about it and I could tell, even then, he felt hopeless.

For a short time my parents tried to reconcile and mom moved back, but the fighting only seemed to intensify and soon the divorce papers were signed and this time it was dad moving out. He moved just 20 minutes away but it may just as well have been 100.

Mom had been a stay at home mom up until then and we quickly found out what it was like to be poor. Our meals were now paid for by food stamps and our clothes were being bought at the thrift store. Even our Thanksgiving turkey was provided by our local church. They would pick out needy people every year and deliver a turkey to their door. We were on the list for a few years until mom eventually found decent work in the mail room of the Nebraska State Capitol building.

While the parents were trying hard to find their way, it appeared the kids were doing the same. Being unattended allowed for some mischief to say the least.

At first I was still lost in my puppet world and was quite oblivious to the changes but eventually I noticed my sister was now surrounded by a different group of friends. Instead of the usual neighborhood kids, there were now teenagers I had never seen before. This new group was pretty scary to me at first. They wore different clothes with t-shirts of rock bands I had never heard of and they had really long hair and seemed kind of dirty.

The other big thing I noticed was they all smoked cigarettes. This was not something I had never seen before. Both of my parents smoked often but it was the first time I had ever seen kids doing it and I was a bit shocked.

The other unusual behavior was the kids would only come over when my mom was gone and would leave before she got back. Since, my mom was gone a lot during this time, our house soon became the gathering place for the type of people parents would warn their kids about. Within weeks, our home went from two parents fighting to a place filled with teens smoking.

SIX

At first my sister made an effort to hide things from my brother and me by taking her friends out to the garage.

My brother Todd took the first bold step out to the garage to see what all the fuss was about. It's kind of like one of those bad B-movie horror films where, one by one, someone goes out to see what the hubbub is only to never return. That was what happened to Todd. He was sucked right into the group and soon he had some new friends as well.

So like the last guy in the B-movie I eventually got up enough nerve or rather curiosity and stepped outside one summer night to see for myself. I remember there were about ten kids outside. Some were in the garage while others were sitting and smoking in the driveway but what I really noticed more than the smoking was the beer each person was holding.

The kids seemed older but I knew no one out there was old enough to be drinking. In addition to the beer I also, for the first time, witnessed various make-out sessions going on. Whatever innocent naivety I had was now forever lost.

Soon after seeing me outside, my sister came up to me and asked me not to say anything to anyone about what was going on. I could not help but notice she was talking to me as if I were a little child and then when my brother joined in I suddenly felt like the baby of the family.

I was shocked to see my sister and brother joking with these people and even more shocked to see them both with beers in their hands.

My emotions were being challenged in ways that were new to me. Suddenly I was more concerned about fitting in than ever before. Within minutes I went from the puppets in my room to trying to be a cool guy in front of people I had never met before.

After a short while I made some excuse and went back inside. But something was different. Something had changed in the way I thought about things. I was now fully aware I was not seen as one of the cool kids and for some strange reason, I now wanted to be one of them.

I'm not sure if it was my flare for dramatics or just a desire to jump right into things but a few days later I took a rather large plunge into the world of attempted coolness.

My mom had some liquor under the kitchen cabinet and I grabbed the first thing I saw. It was a tall bottle of tequila and I poured six small shot glass sized cups. As I sat there at the kitchen table with the cups in front of me, my brother and sister asked me what I was doing.

"I'm going to get drunk." I said with as much cool and calm as I could muster up.

And then I took cup number one and gulped it.

Lesson learned; tequila should not be gulped. My face began contorting into expressions I didn't know I had. Suddenly it felt like ice cold air was rushing through every hole in my body but yet I was sweating at the same time. My siblings waited for a reaction so I tried to say,

"Now for cup number two"

But I think it came out "oh my God!"

I took the second cup a bit slower and had gotten the hang of the taste by the third although I never did master the reflex of wanting to vomit with each sip.

Sixth cup down and I waited. I knew I should be feeling something but was unsure what that feeling would be. I actually didn't even know I was drunk until I noticed my sister was pulling me up off the kitchen floor. I would use the floor as a guide for when to stop drinking from then on but for now, I was ready to get the attention and show the world Trever was now a cool guy.

Fortunately I had my brother and sister to help show me off to their friends. After all, I had just drunk a half bottle of tequila and this was bragging rights for even them.

I faintly remember stumbling around the town while my new-found peer group laughed at my actions. We went to the park which was the local hang out for ne'er-do-wells when they weren't hanging out at my house. I was the life of that party. People kept asking me how I felt and telling me I was wasted. Of course, by this time no one had to tell me I was wasted. After all, I could see air, which even at ten I knew was unusual in the summer time. Besides, this was not like air coming out of people's mouths but rather the air that is all around us. Some people see pink elephants; I saw air.

As the hippies laughed, I really felt like I had graduated from being the puppet dork to the new cool kid in town. At least I felt that way until throwing up on one of my sister's friends. I'm not sure which one it was. (The air was blocking my vision.) And it didn't end there. One full hour of mirthfulness and inebriation had now turned into multiple hours of vomiting and dry heaves. Hours that unfortunately elapsed into the time my mother came home with her friends.

As much as one tries to act sober, it is never very convincing when lying on the bathroom floor, resting one arm in the toilet. My mother figured out right away what had happened and my brother and sister gladly filled her in on the details. I was shocked at how quickly they turned on me. I guess they saw the confrontation with my mom just as entertaining as parading me in front of their friends.

Mom tried to lecture me but I was too indisposed to hear anything so she left me to literally choke on things for a while. By the time evening rolled around I was able to crawl out of the bathroom. Mom was sitting in the living room asking if I had learned a lesson. I groaned and assured her I would never do anything like that again and she took my word for it.

Even then, I knew I was going to drink again. The hour of intoxication just felt too good and I absolutely loved the attention I got. I mean, let's face it, Pebbles made a good audience but she didn't laugh like these kids did. From that moment on, I was hooked.

I held back on the hard liquor for a while and started drinking beer. I soon learned it was the easiest thing to obtain through either someone's older brother or a store clerk that was more concerned with being cool than obeying the law.

I soon began to hang around my brother and his new-found friends. There were a few of them but the main ones were Jeff and Paul (not the Mormon), two brothers just about a year older than us, but who had plenty of experience with alcohol thanks to their two older brothers.

I think my brother and I found common ground with Jeff and Paul because they too were brothers that fought as much as we did. Jeff was a year younger than Paul but they were both in the same grade and felt annoyed and bothered by each other often.

Jeff was always trying his best to be a lady's man but sadly, like the rest of us, he never really had any ladies to pull it off. He would often try to court some poor girl by singing Zeppelin songs way off key and grossing them out with his overpowering cigarette breath.

Paul was known for doing some pretty dumb things when intoxicated like the time someone told him he could squeeze a light bulb in his hand as hard as he wanted but it wouldn't break due to equal pressure. Paul put it to the test and became the joke of the week. I'd bet he still has the twenty or so tiny little scars on his hand to prove the equal pressure theory wrong.

So what do a failed Casanova, a bulb squeezer, and a former puppeteer have in common? We had drugs.

I think my brother was a bit acrimonious when I began to tag along with him and his friends. Actually I think he downright hated it. After all, I was the puppet nerd but I was also his bully and beyond that, I was more outgoing than he was. Todd had some shyness issues when we were younger and he was often known as the quiet one. I think he resented the fact I could start up and hog nearly every conversation.

I always felt the need to take the spot light. When I did puppet shows for my grandmother she seemed to truly think I had talent. Unfortunately, the only role I played now was the role of a pothead and troublemaker. I was now embarrassed of my puppetry past and wanted to make sure everyone knew I was a cool guy. I began acting out in class by verbally assaulting my teachers and scaring the hell out of my fellow students.

There was a case with one teacher where the verbal assault turned physical. It was in seventh grade. I had worn down Mrs. Webber with several verbal attacks and she could not take it anymore and told me to go to the principal's office. When I refused she attempted to pull me out of my chair and instinctively I slugged her in the stomach.

She hunched over and some kids laughed while a few others screamed. I felt like a real cool guy for about five minutes until the high school principle came to the door. Mrs. Webber jumped right past the junior high guy and went straight to the 6′ 3″ no nonsense high school principle. Now I felt like hunching over.

The walk to detention was pretty scary. The

principle walked ahead of me while I noticed the difference in our height as my head only came up to his butt.

He never even said a word and just marched me to detention where I spent the rest of the week. By Monday I was in a different class. Instead of Mrs. Webber, I had a teacher with a reputation of duct taping mouths shut when kids talked too much. I never hit a teacher again but it was not the last time I ever hit.

When I was in grade school, even though I was playing with puppets, I was a bully. There were two people in particular I would terrorize; John and Stacy. To this day I do not know why they were picked. Neither of them did anything to me and I would say both were very nice people. I hated the bully I was but for some reason I could not seem to stop.

A few years back I found John on Facebook and wrote him a letter of apology. He gracefully forgave me and said he was doing well. I need to apologize to Stacy as well, but so far, I have not been able to locate her.

I found by using drugs and hanging around other scary people I no longer had to resort to violence. I only had to play the part. All my acting talents were focused on the role of a mean drug using jerk and I used sarcasm to belittle and dehumanize people and I found I was quite good at it.

My quick wit proved time and again to be no match for anyone I took on and I didn't care if you were a student, a teacher, a principle, or a parent. I remember one angry father trying to throw a bicycle at me in a park because I continued to make fun of his weight.

I was truly an asshole to people and played the part very well but I was never able to rid myself of the guilt of my actions. No matter how much alcohol or marijuana I took, I was never able to fully escape feelings I had and the one that seemed to trouble me more than any was sadness.

They say the child in you never leaves and for me that child was in his room with his dog or putting on puppet shows for his grandma and I secretly missed him a great deal. But it seemed the more I missed that child, the more I ran from him.

My drug and alcohol usage grew and by the age of 12 I could down a twelve pack without flinching. I only wish I could say I could do it without throwing up.

I have never drank one beer, never been tipsy, never had wine or fancy drinks of any kind. Vodka became a favorite of mine just because I thought it was cool to tell people I was drinking it. The taste always knocked me on my butt but it got me drunk fast and I was even able to guzzle that after a while.

The drinking and drug usage became my identity. I dressed like a hippy and grew my hair out long. I wanted it to grow like Jim Morrison's, but my curly hairs made me look more like a white Jimmi Hendrix which also gave me a sense of pride.

The time and energy I spent on drugs and alcohol cost me many things. I did not have any real friends other than the ones I used with and we only talked about drugs and rock and roll. I deliberately left out the first part of that fine American saying. There was no sex for me and I may have been one of the few and maybe only virgins in my group, although it's difficult to tell.

Everyone had their stories and neither of us could trust the other. As for me there were not any offers and I surely did not know much about sex. Most of the kids I hung around were quite older and many of them talked about their wild nights but I wasn't sure what they meant by certain parts of the conversation and I surely wasn't going to ask.

The summer I turned 13 did open my eyes to some things. I remember there was a foster girl living with some family and she soon began hanging out with the drug group.

For some reason she found me attractive and told me so, many times, to the shock of others. She was quite a bit older, a junior in high school I believe, and was even dating one of the local hunks. But one summer day she arrived at my house and we started to kiss. A little bit later she took off her shirt and for the first time I knew what being heterosexual was really all about.

By the next school year I drank and smoked more than ever and failed the eighth grade. I had a chance to make up the school credits by going to summer school but I failed that too. I found the drug users there and we skipped class and got high instead.

By the time I was 14 I was smoking a pack of cigarettes and getting drunk, stoned, or both every day. Every morning I got out of bed, took a shower, and threw up. I was massively underweight. At first I was elated not to be chubby again but I think I was more chemical than person. I also carried more guilt and sadness than ever before. The child inside me still wanted out but I continued to push him down.

SEVEN

I don't remember what time of year it was but I am guessing it was summer. Like many times before, I had snuck out all night to hang with my doped-up friends. We had vodka and Coca-Cola and a few joints between us and spent the night in the park, sitting on the roof of the swimming pool and throwing empty bottles into the water.

I was still out of sorts by the next morning when I came home to find my mother waiting for me. She told me to call my father. I thought it was unusual she did not yell or even act mad about me being out all night and it was very unusual to be calling my dad like this.

When he answered the phone I tried to act as chipper as I could but he immediately told me everyone was looking for me during the night. He then told me my grandma had died of a heart attack.

I felt so weak I did not know what to say. All I could think about was my grandma heading to Heaven in the night and looking down to see me stoned out of my mind.

At first I couldn't even cry about it. I was still so high I did not feel much of anything but the shock soon sobered me up and before long I was in my room bawling my eyes out.

My dog Pebbles came in and I held her and wished I had never shut out the child that held those puppets and put on those shows. I would give anything to do them again for my grandma if I only had the chance but that chance was now gone. She died in bed while I was stoned.

I'd love to say I sobered up after that but the drug and alcohol usage actually increased as did my meanness. I began to push everyone away. I fought with the people I was using with and what seemed like a permanent scowl affixed itself to my face. No matter how much I wanted to go back to who I was; there was no chance I could. Or at least, that is what I thought.

In a surprising twist, my mom began to show she had other plans. There was an older kid we would sometimes get high with named Rodney and apparently Rodney got into some trouble and was sent to an inpatient treatment center for drug and alcohol addiction.

We all thought it was as if Rodney was going to prison and the night before he left, his friends did their best to make sure he had enough drugs, alcohol, and sex to sustain him for the 30 to 45 days he would be gone.

Soon after he left, it seemed life just went on as usual. We all continued to smoke and drink and I don't even recall anyone even saying anything about Rodney being gone. It's as if no one even missed him at all. Nothing changed. Well, almost nothing.

It seems while Rodney was gone, my mother had a conversation with Rodney's mom about the treatment process. Not only did Rodney's mom talk about treatment but she also talked about Alanon and something called tough love. Both of these entities taught my mom how to be stronger and do things out of love that she may have considered harsh at one time.

She began to wait up for us and make surprise visits to the park where we hung out. One time she showed up at the house when we thought she was in Lincoln shopping. We just happened to be attempting to dry about 5 pounds of marijuana in the oven.

A week before mom had put a bolt lock on her bedroom door because we would often steal money from her. As a result of the lock we quickly became broke and could not find the money to buy drugs. In desperation, we went to a local field to try to harvest our own.

We convinced ourselves the marijuana was growing in rows so obviously it was planted by a dealer. The truth was it was common ditch weed. That's marijuana without its precious tetrahydrocannabinol, also known as THC. That's the stuff that gets you high and it is also the stuff missing from the billions of marijuana weeds growing in the USA but as I said before, we were desperate to try anything and we did not count on my mother coming home.

As soon as she came in the back door the crowd of drug hungry hippies ran out the front door. I stayed behind.

I was always the one that stayed back while the others ran off. My puppets may have been in boxes but my creative side was still in full use as a bullshit artist. Whether it was angry neighbors, liquor store clerks, or even police officers, I could talk my way out of any situation through manipulation, acting, and bold-faced lying. When it came to freeing ourselves from certain doom, I was the hero who saved the day.

At first I thought I would tell her we were doing a scientific experiment. Then I thought I could say the stove wasn't working so we decide to cook our hotdogs by starting a small fire.

Eventually I decided the best argument would be that we saw the marijuana growing on the side of the road and decided to destroy it before innocent children could get their hands on it.

The new strong person that seemed to take over my mother's mind was starting to become a bit of a challenge. She would no longer buy any of my excuses and of course having a house smell like a small forest fire did not help any of my lies.

Now instead of arguing with me like I wanted her to do, she would merely say the word "no." This was difficult. In an argument, I have more openings to play against her emotions and more opportunities to manipulate, lie, and get my way. Just saying a calm "no" totally disrupted my game plan and I found myself often filled with rage over it.

I remember on one occasion being red in the face with every single muscle flexed as my mother just smiled and said "No." I think her smiles were due to the topic of the attempted argument. I wanted to be a carnie.

There was a traveling carnival in town for the 4th of July weekend and I wanted to quit school and run away with them.

I really could care less about the job of being a carnival guy but I hated school and always felt stupid when it came to academics. Thankfully, my mom did not back down and the carnival left without me.

The argument that changed my life followed another late night of partying. For some reason we had a rather large amount of marijuana (not from the ditch) and vodka and I was testing my limits with both. Within an hour I was beyond my limits and parading around like a king.

Someone brought a bicycle and I hopped on telling everyone I could do tricks but it seemed the only trick I knew was how to flip myself into the pavement and tear a large and deep gash into my wrist. Girls were turning away in fright and boys were telling me I should go to the doctor. I had no idea what anyone was talking about because I could not feel a thing. I could not see anything either. The high I was feeling had also caused my eyes to see nothing but a dark blur.

Shortly after the bike ride I stumbled off behind a shed and passed out for a short time and woke up with a girl sitting down beside me. This girl had a bad reputation as being easy with the boys but no boy ever wanted to admit to being with her. She was not considered to be very attractive.

She was asking me if my wrist was okay. I sat up and told her I had no idea what she was talking about and then asked her for a cigarette. She gave me one and then started to check her pockets for a lighter. Then, with all my chivalry, I told her I would help her look and I began feeling her up and down and kissed her.

I know it did not go any further because in less than a minute Jeff came around the corner of the shed singing "American Woman" by the Guess Who. He told us it was 3 am and everyone was taking off. Tomorrow was a school day and some of the people there actually wanted to get some sleep so they could hit the books.

Somebody helped me up and I bummed another cigarette and began to stagger home. It always amazed me no matter how gone I was I could always find my way back to the house. I guess it was because it was such a small town and we always partied at the same few places; the park, Jeff and Paul's house, or even this old run down pool room where the owner would turn the other way if we shared what we had.

On a side note, that pool room was the first place I got hit so hard across the face, I actually swung around in a full circle like they do in the movies.

I learned being drunk can sometimes lead to challenging people much bigger than you and even though you spin, you do not feel the impact of any punch until the next day when you sober up, just like I had not felt anything wrong with my wrist as I stumbled in the door with dried blood on my shirt and pants.

In the past I could easily sneak in and collapse in my bed but that tough love stuff had taught my mom the benefits of staying up and seeing firsthand what was going on. She was in the kitchen when I came in the back door.

I don't remember exactly what was said, but I know it started with my mom asking me where I had been and ended with me throwing out every kind of swear word and demeaning thing I could say to my mom. I stumbled into my room as she was saying we would be talking about this when I was sober.

I passed out on my bed and woke up the next morning still in the blood-stained clothes I wore the night before. It took a while to remember what had happened, but the pain came immediately as I discovered my blood had dried my wrist to my sheets. I winced as I pulled it apart and began to plan my scheme for getting out of the dog house with my mom.

Sometimes when people are drunk they have blackouts causing them to forget everything that happened the night before and then there were moments like these when one wishes they did not remember the things that happened the night before.

The first thing I remembered was how I yelled at my mom and I knew I had to come up with a plan that would eliminate the ability for her to be angry about the night before. What I needed was for her to actually feel sorry for me and quickly forgive me rather than be angry and try to punish me.

I then came up with the perfect plan. I rehearsed the words as I took a shower, changed into some clean clothes and stuck a Band-Aid on my wrist. The house was its usual bustle on a school day as people were flying to get going. My mom was getting her things together for work when I came out and set my con into motion. I placed my arm around her shoulder.

"Mom," I said in my softest and most caring voice, "I am so sorry about last night and I have been thinking a lot about my behavior lately. I am worried I may have a problem with drugs and alcohol."

I thought this approach was brilliant. I knew my mom had been talking with Rodney's mom and I also knew he was now being called a drug addict and an alcoholic. But what I also knew was Rodney was using drugs the minute he got back and partying like nothing had ever been wrong.

In my head I thought I would play the addict card and my mom would then be sympathetic, as if I just told her I had cancer, and ease off any thought of a punishment. Maybe she might bring home some pamphlets on teen issues or something and that would be that.

But that was not that. It seems mom had not only been talking with Rodney's mom but also to some experts in the field of addiction and she was ready for me.

"I think you have a problem too." She said in such a calm voice it sent shivers down my spine. "As a matter of fact, I just made you an appointment for an evaluation tonight."

For a minute I thought I was still drunk because I did not understand a word she just said. All I could do was nod and stay true to my original façade.

"I'll be here when you get home from school." She said with full assuredness.

I was dazed as I headed out the door wondering what an evaluation was and whether or not it was I who had walked into a lie this time.

By the time I had arrived at school I was convinced my mom was delivering an empty threat to scare me straight and if I played along I may get the reprieve I needed to avoid any more "tough love."

There was no time to think about this during the school day as it turns out I was a hero. Apparently word of my sexual escapades from the night before had spread into rumors of a full blown sexual encounter and even though the girl had the reputation of being easy and unattractive, she was two grades above me and that made me a practical stallion in my grade. Naturally, I let the rumors fester and just gave a coy smile when anyone asked me about it.

By the time I got home I was feeling like a confident stud that could do no wrong and I was even kind of proud of my good-for-nothing ways. I felt like a tough guy. I felt cool. I even felt ready to take my mom to task and call her bluff by playing right into her hands.

As she promised, she was waiting for me when I got home and told me she was ready to take me for my evaluation. I looked at her right in the eye and said I was all set to go. She took the bluff a step further and told me to get in the car. I got in the car and within moments we were heading to Lincoln and I knew I was in trouble.

EIGHT

It was a silent ride to the treatment center. I'm not sure either of us knew really what to say to each other. Mom was new at the tough love stuff and I was totally caught off guard by the actions being taken.

The building we drove up to looked like it had been built in the 1920's. It was tall with many old windows and right next to it was Lincoln General Hospital. I had no idea why a place like this would be next to a hospital but I did not give it much thought. I was still trying to figure out what an evaluation was.

We sat down in an old dingy waiting room for just minutes before a young man came to get us. He walked us down a dimly lit hallway and talked with my mom for a very short time before asking me to join him alone in his office.

He sat behind a very large desk. It was intimidating, but he wasn't. He was very down to earth and just started to ask me questions about my drug usage like how often I drank and which drugs I had used.

This was one of the times I was really aware of my brain having an argument with my heart. My brain was telling me to lie and tell this man nothing that could get me into trouble but my heart was pushing me to tell the honest truth.

My heart won and for some reason I was not only answering the man's questions, I was also adding in things he may have forgot to ask about. The man just sat there behind the large desk as I spilled my guts out and persecuted myself before him. He did not seem startled in the least. As a matter of fact, I would say he even looked bored at times but after I was finished he leaned over the big desk and looked at me in the eyes and said,

"Well Trever, from what you have told me, I would say you are an alcoholic and a drug addict."

"I'm a what?" I asked with all seriousness.

And then he told me the amount of times I used and the trouble it has brought me were signs of a serious problem. He then said now that they know how much I used drugs it was time to find out why I used them. And then he said the really big thing.

"I am going to recommend inpatient treatment."

I was truly stunned but deep down inside I also felt relieved. I didn't know why at the time but, under all the long hair and tough looks, the real me was still there and still longed for the days of being in my room with my dog and playing with those puppets. But I was also afraid those days were gone forever.

The date was set. I would have four days before going into treatment and like Rodney before me I had plenty of drugs and alcohol for those four days. Naturally, I was hoping for the sex as well but there were no offers at the time. It also seemed my mom curbed the tough love during that time as well. I was like a prisoner heading to the electric chair and everyone wanted to make sure I got in my last meal.

By the time I got to treatment I felt as if my mouth would forever taste like the end of a joint and I would be burping up cheap beer for the rest of my life. But when we walked in the door I immediately sobered up.

Before I actually went into the place I would be calling home for the next 60 days, I had to have a talk with the head person that ran the place. Her name was Lu and she was as mean as they come. Her bluntness often made you feel as if you had just been hit by a two-by-four. Before I even sat down she started in.

"Why do you wear that hat?"

Ever since I began using drugs I started to wear English driving caps, or "Newsboys" as some would call them. I saw an older kid wearing one once and I thought it looked cool so I was never seen without one.

"Do you wear it to be cool?" asked Lu.

Amazing. I had not been in her office for a minute and she was already reading me like a book.

"No." I answered with an attempt to stop shaking, "I just like them."

"You are not going to be wearing it here." She said firmly.

I looked at my mom and noticed a faint grin on her face as Lu continued to grill me.

"Are you sexually active?" she asked without blinking.

I was fourteen and had never heard this phrase

before so all I could offer was a dumbfounded look.

"Have you ever had sex?" She asked.

Normally if I was asked this I would make some sarcastic remark to hide the fact I was still a virgin but in this case I was betting the truth would help me.

"No, I have not." I said with my best innocent looking face.

"Good." She slammed back, "because there is no f#@king in treatment."

This expletive was not new to me. Around my using friends I heard it and said it all the time but this was the first time I had ever heard it in a way that made me want to blush. My mom continued to grin.

After more grilling and a search through my pockets and bags I was brought to a small building that sat right across the big building where I had my evaluation.

I found out the big building was primarily used for adults and the small building I was entering was used for kids. There were about 25 in this building ranging in age from 12 to 19. Some were from Lincoln but many were from all over the state. Some were brought in by their parents and others were brought in by a court order. There were even some facing possible jail times, even if they went through treatment with flying colors. There were thieves, fighters, drunk drivers, wards of the state, foster kids, you name it. I immediately felt humbled by some of the impressive rap sheets I was hearing from the others.

As tough as these kids were, it seemed everyone had been chopped down a few pegs by the vicious

Lu and even the kids with violent records were fearful of her. I distinctly remember seeing her bring a tough guy to tears. He was being a bit threatening and by the time she was finished with him he was bawling his eyes out and telling us how much shame he felt for the things he had done in his life.

That was really what treatment was all about. Finding the reasons we all used drugs and facing the things we were trying to escape from. For me it was insecurities. I had them bad and would do anything to try to make myself come off better than I thought I was.

I also had to face my parents and tell them how angry I was for the way I was treated by them. I was able to sit down with my mom face-to-face and tell her all the things she did that made me angry and then apologize for all the things I had done to her. It was a tearful session ending with a hug and made me feel closer to my mom than ever before.

I could talk about the abuse and anger to my counselor but I couldn't talk these things over with my dad. He just scared me too much and I struggled with the feelings of being a disappointment to him.

Another topic that was discussed quite a bit was spirituality. There was a chaplain on staff and he would meet with us to discuss our faith. The treatment center used the 12 steps of Alcoholics Anonymous and a great deal of those steps referred to believing in a power greater than ourselves and relying on that power to restore us to a better place than the mess we had all gotten ourselves into.

The idea of asking God for help fascinated and

troubled me. I had always believed in God but knew nothing about him and often found myself feeling he was probably pretty disappointed in me and had given up on me long ago.

The feelings of my Grandma's last day on earth continued to haunt me and I felt undeserving of anything God had to offer me. After all, I had lied to many people for so long and done many things, but God always knew.

I became superstitious after my grandmother's death and would never get high or drunk unless there was something over me like a roof or even trees. It was my way of hiding my sins from God but no matter how much I rationalized things, I always knew that God saw everything and was very unhappy.

For weeks in treatment I struggled with the thought of God actually forgiving me and then something happened that really was a changing point for my recovery. During the evenings the staff would walk us all a block down the road to this old house that had been converted into a place where AA meetings were held several times a week.

In some meetings we would sit and listen to a speaker tell their story of how they got addicted and how they got sober. In other meetings a topic would be picked and then discussed by everyone there. For these meetings we would all sit in a circle and take turns commenting on the topic.

That night the topic was on a higher power. Higher power is a phrase used instead of God because some have different beliefs as in the case at this meeting. Some people talked about worshiping crystals which was popular at the time and another person worshiped the wind. One man told us he had trouble believing in anything so his higher power was a living room chair. When it came my turn, I apparently remembered something from Sunday school and said I believed in God and in Jesus Christ. My problem was whether or not they believed in me.

As the meeting came to an end, people began to socialize and drink coffee that tasted like it had been brewed a few years back. I sat in my chair alone and in deep thought.

I had just told people my higher power was Jesus Christ and yet I knew nothing about God and even doubted if God gave a care about me in the first place. Why did I even say I believed in Jesus Christ? I guess it was the only name I knew when it came to religion.

But truthfully I had no idea who Jesus was. I remember there were times I even felt awkward saying his name out loud. To me the name Jesus sounded weak and like something from a children's book. It was all part of the God stuff meant for others and not for me. And yet here I was proclaiming my faith to Jesus as if I considered him to be an old friend of the family.

I was without answers and for the first time in my life I prayed. It was a simple prayer.

I just said, "God, are you there?"

And in that moment I felt a hand placed upon my shoulder. It was firm and comforting at the same time. It startled me and I turned to see who was there but realized I was sitting against a wall. I also realized even though no one was there, the feeling of the hand on my shoulder was still there and to my shock, I even felt the hand squeeze my shoulder.

I jumped up and began pacing and wondering what had just happened. The most amazing thing about that hand was how comforting it felt and even as I paced the floor I did not lose that feeling. I began to smile and could not stop smiling the rest of the night.

The next day I told everyone about it. My counselor, my roommates, and I also talked about it in one of our small group sessions. People would smile and encourage me but no one showed as much excitement as I had. At first that bothered me but then I realized how much more personal it made things.

God had touched me and comforted me in a way that was meant for just me. Until then, I never knew people could experience God in very personal ways and for me, this personal touch told me it was not too late for me to return to the person I was before drugs had taken over.

I started working very hard on my recovery and I began helping others with theirs by giving feedback in small groups or talking with them over dinner. I became the treatment kid. The staff talked about the miraculous change in me and told me how they were about to give up on me but now felt I was a huge success.

In the days following I called the people I used to get drunk and stoned with, telling them I could no longer hang out with them. I did not want to have the same fate as Rodney and come back to the same group only to begin again with drugs and alcohol. I was determined to remain drug and alcohol free for the rest of my life.

One might think I would forever wave a Christian banner and forever thank Jesus for my second chance but for some reason I quickly forgot all about Him.

NINE

Getting out was a bit scary. I had been in treatment from November 2nd to December 30th. I spent Thanksgiving and Christmas away from my family and for two months I learned to live without the use of chemicals. But it was December 30th and that meant that the biggest drinking day was just 24 hours away.

To help me get going in the real world, my counselor set me up with a sponsor. In AA a sponsor is someone with more sobriety than you and hopefully some more wisdom. The sponsor I was teamed up with was both of those in many ways.

His name was Ben and he was about five years older than me. Ben took me under his wing right away and I spent New Year's Eve hanging out with him and his friends. They were all sober and we started the night drinking coffee and talking. He asked me what I did. I had no idea what he meant by this so I told him I did nothing. He told me he played drums and before long we were in some guy's basement watching Ben do a hippy impression of Buddy Rich.

After that Ben and his gang took me to the local Native American Center where an A.A. dance was going on. I had never seen such a mix of culture in my life. In addition to Native Americans, there were African Americans, Mexicans, Asians, and even a few white people.

Scary looking, leather wearing bikers joked around with nerdy guys wearing elbow patched suit jackets. Being from a small town of one color and culture, this was an eye opener and a wonderful one at that.

Ben's girlfriend was Native American and I soon discovered she was the happy leader of the group, always making sure we were all having fun and smiling.

She asked me if I could dance and before I answered she pulled me out on the floor while the disc jockey played Hollywood Nights by Bob Seger. I tried my best to dance but soon learned, no matter how many different cultures are in a room together, everyone laughs when you dance like a goof. I saw it as another step toward global peace.

Ben and his peers were a great fit for me but they were not your typical teens. In the 50's they would have been beatniks, in the seventies they would have been hippies, but we were in the eighties so I have no idea what I would call them. Perhaps I would refer to them as intellectuals. While other kids were listening to the latest pops songs and watching MTV this group was going out for coffee and reading books.

I quickly became a fan of the lifestyle. I loved talking politics, religion, and sharing aspirations for what we wanted to do with our lives. When it came to politics, we hated government and trusted no one. When it came to religion, everyone was an atheist. Everyone, that is, but me. I still claimed to be a Christian even though I had yet to be in a church or do anything resembling a religious act.

The memory of the touch on my shoulder was tucked back somewhere and while I had experienced Jesus, I was still going to do things my way. I was an intellectual. I was now a deep thinker.

In addition to being a drummer and a deep thinker, Ben was also an artist. I used to sit for hours and watch him and a fellow artist by the name of Jeff use pens and pencils to create worlds from empty sheets of paper. Ben would draw mystical wizards pulling dragons from copper kettles while Jeff would draw cartoons and caricatures of the people at the coffee shop. The creativity they both had was inspiring.

Along with Ben and Jeff, there was Jim who was the smartest one of the group and Ben's sister Mindy, who really taught me how to be great friends with a girl without having any other expectations. (A lesson I would need to relearn over and over again.)

When I wasn't with Ben's group I was in Aftercare—a small group that met at the treatment center every day that included newly sober teens. It was a great support group and a good place to socialize but there was sadness to it as well.

Being a part of a group like this allowed you to see the statistics of the success in sobriety close up. Just as you got close to someone you would find out the next day they left the group and went back to their drugs.

I knew I did not want to be one of the ones lost. I kept away from my old using peers and hangouts and spent nearly every day with Ben and his friends.

I was also becoming a public speaker. Around 1984 sobriety became the hot topic of many schools and several of them invited me out to speak at assemblies to students of all ages.

I traveled all over the state with counselors and experts on drugs and alcohol and gave my story. I was asked to speak to the students of my own school. It set the record straight that I was no longer the kid they knew from before and many of the ones who feared me became my friends.

By the time I was 15 I got a job at the local grocery store. It was there I met Cyler. Cyler was a college student with a sense of humor that was more than eye opening for me.

He looked like Ritchie Cunningham from Happy Days but reminded me of Bill Cosby in the way he would tell stories about his childhood.

Cyler's stories would leave me in tears with laughter. It was a new kind of high and I wanted more.

I began to hang around Cyler after work. He was always riding his bicycle on long distance rides down the highway and as soon as I got enough money saved, I bought a bike, and was riding right beside him. We would ride about 25 miles from the town of Waverly to Lincoln and then ride around Lincoln for hours before taking the 25 mile ride back

It was really during this time that I began to rediscover my sense of humor. First it was Cyler and the guys from the store and then it was Ben and his intellectual friends. They said I had an intelligent wit and some said it reminded them of Groucho Marx.

The comparison to Groucho would not turn out to be as much of a compliment as I thought. While someone like Groucho is hilarious when you are watching him from the audience's perspective, it can be quite hurtful when the insults and sarcasm are aimed at friends.

In my attempts to be funny I realized that I still had the dark side in me that often came out in my drug using days. I would sometimes make fun of a person's clothing, hairstyle, or the way they talked. Close friends soon began to point it out to me and I struggled to curb the nasty humor and be nicer.

I got a chance to practice my nice side after my dad got remarried and had a daughter named Melissa. She was such a cute child and I was thrilled to have a younger sister.

It was important to me to be a good older brother to Melissa. I did not want her to grow up in a world of chaos like her siblings did.

When she was little, Melissa loved to swim and I would take her to the pool. I was feeling too cool at the time to put on a suit and swim with her so I would sit on a bench. While Melissa swam with her friends, she would look over to make sure I was watching. I would wave and encourage her to have fun.

Sometimes while Melissa was preoccupied with her friends I would sneak peeks at the older girls in bikinis. I was shocked one day to see one of my old English teachers sunbathing by the pool. The way she glistened in the sun made me wish I had been a lot nicer to her in the classroom.

In time I started to see tension building between my dad and his new wife. Soon they were divorced and Melissa ended up staying with her mom. I did not see her as much after that.

Like his marriage to my mom, my dad again, ended up alone. As the years went by, the fear of my dad began to subside and in its place was a new feeling. I began to pity him.

TEN

I was 5 years sober when I turned 19. I moved to Lincoln and started working at the place I went through treatment. My job was helping out with the kids between their counseling sessions. I would talk with them and take them to dinner and to AA meetings. Getting the job was pretty easy being that Ben and Jim already worked there.

In recent years Jim and I had become very good friends. He shared my sense of humor and laughed at all my jokes so it was a pleasure to hang out with him. In addition to Jim, I became good friends with a fellow student from High School by the name of Rich and soon the three of us were inseparable.

Being introduced to a creative group after treatment helped to nurture my own creativity and by the time I was working at the treatment center I was also doing standup comedy at some local clubs in Lincoln and Omaha. I loved anything to do with comedy and just being in the clubs was euphoric.

I was only 19 but hanging out with some of the best touring comedians I had ever seen and I felt like one of them. We talked the same language and became this creative circle of comics, all laughing and enjoying each other's artistry.

Oddly enough the first standup routine I wrote was about Jesus Christ. It was about the reactions from others as he was growing up as the son of God. I thought it would be funny to show envy in his school mates and mentioned how Joseph was insecure about being just a stepdad.

I meant no disrespect by the routine and told it in a very respectful way. However some audience members were offended because they thought I was making fun of Christians. Then some audience members were offended because I was a Christian. I dropped the joke in the first year.

The comics I found the most enjoyable were the ones who never told a dirty joke or even swore on stage. One comic told me anyone can tell a dirty joke and get a room filled with drunks to laugh but when you can do the same while being clean the whole time, you can call yourself a true comedian. I took her words to heart and never did a routine that wasn't clean.

The biggest lesson I learned was in order to be successful in comedy you had to stand behind your craft. You had to be confident in what you were doing and if you weren't you had to be able to fake it. If an audience can tell you are insecure they will eat you alive.

I was in a club in Omaha and started to do my routine when, for the first time, a table full of drunks started to heckle me. I learned that night that fear could actually be a trusted friend. You always hear about people doing heroic things when they are frightened and stories referring to the fight or flight scenario. That night was when I knew for sure I was a fight kind of guy.

The practiced routine was tossed to the side and the ad lib work began. It started with some sarcasm to put the drunks in their place but then turned to talking with the audience. I would carry on conversations with people at random and come up with funny comments. Before I knew it I won over the hecklers and the whole club was laughing at everything I said. From that moment on I never used a practiced routine again and stuck to saying whatever came off the top my head.

Comedy gave me such a high but it also worked like a drug because once I left the stage I was miserable. No matter how great a night I would have, I always went home hating myself and thinking the worst about my performance.

After a few months of working at the treatment center I was introduced to the recreational therapist. She was quite beautiful with long blond hair that really stood out next to her eyes. She was three years older than me and from what I was told she had a bit of a wild side but nevertheless I asked her out and when she said yes I thought I was in love.

I was so excited that someone wanted to actually go out with me I forgot it was the first time I had ever asked anyone. And that was not the only first. After a month of dating I was no longer a virgin and we were living together.

I soon discovered there was an intense moodiness to my new girlfriend and soon I was getting yelled at every day. Sometimes it would be for legitimate reasons like leaving the toilet seat up but other times it would be for minor things like shutting a mouse tail in a drawer.

We had a terrible mouse problem in our first house and I will be the first to admit they give me the creeps. My girlfriend was raised on a farm and I guess they get used to them there but for me it was a terrible time and I would find them everywhere.

I was at our desk paying bills one afternoon when I opened a drawer for a stamp and found a fat mouse eating them. I slammed the door shut quick and discovered I also slammed the mouse's tail in the drawer. I had no idea what to do and paced the floor for a while trying to think of a way out of my new predicament.

I knew I couldn't just open the drawer again but I also could not pay the bills while this creepy tail continued to wiggle about. After about an hour more of pacing I noticed the tail was no longer wiggling. I began to wonder if somehow the mouse had separated from the tail so I formed a plan to find out using the only resources I could find.

Wearing oven mitts on both hands and holding a large set of tongs from our grill I squeezed the tail just enough to hear little feet scrambling from inside the desk.

It was then I knew I was facing a moment separating men from boys and called my neighbor for help. He too was an old farmer and told me not to panic. He wasn't panicking but rather trying to keep himself from laughing.

Within minutes he came through the door like Batman and grabbed the tail with one bare hand while opening the drawer with the other. The mouse and I both began to squirm and crap ourselves as my neighbor carried it out the front door.

A second later he came in and told me everything was taken care of. Without a flinch my neighbor told me he smacked the mouse against a rock and threw it in my outside trash can. As he left, I felt weak in the knees and then realized I was still wearing the oven mitts on my hands.

After that my girlfriend no longer called me Trever but took to calling me "Shit for Brains." I was convinced this was the happiest I was ever going to be so I asked her to marry me.

We had the traditional wedding and moved into a two bedroom rental property. I convinced myself that all was well and then I lost my job at the treatment center. They decided to combine the youth with the adults and share a building so they cut staff by seniority. I was the last to go and soon found myself working at a taco place.

The stand-up comedy was a good paying gig but the gigs were few and far. I was married and trying to make my life into that traditional home you see on the hallmark commercials but felt as if I was failing in every way. But soon there would be a light at the end of the tunnel.

What I didn't know was that the light would eventually burn.

ELEVEN

I was in the middle of my job asking people if they would like some hot sauce packets with their tacos when Jenny, a friend of mine from high school came in. She and I had been in some drama clubs together and I had heard she was now working at a radio station in town.

I was a bit embarrassed to be seen behind the taco counter. Here she was in an actual career and here I was getting greased up from the deep fat fryer.

Jenny had gone to college right after high school and earned a degree in broadcasting. She was now making something of herself. I missed the boat for college. Actually to be honest, I never even tried to get on board.

Since my using days I never felt very smart. I knew I had some street sense but I was always been insecure when it came to academics. In later years a few I.Q. tests would show I was above average but back then even the thought of a test would leave me in a cold sweat.

College students became a phobia of mine. I truly was afraid of them. I always felt they were smarter and just plain better than me and higher academics would never have a place for me.

Anyway, back to the tacos. As much as I wanted to hide from Jenny I could not. I was posted that day at the order board and Jenny was next in line.

It was foolish to be embarrassed in front of Jenny. She was one of the truly nicest people anyone could meet. I say truly because we all know people that are nice to your face and then rip your face apart as soon as they are behind your back. I realize this statement sounds impossible but I have seen it none the less.

Jenny was an outspoken Christian. She didn't preach fire and brimstone. She just talked about her love for Jesus and her neighbor. I remember being so curious about her attitude toward life and secretly wanted what she had.

She ignored her taco order and the fact that I was taking it and showed genuine excitement to see me. We played catch up for just a short time and she told me about her job working for a local broadcasting company that owned three stations.

There was an AM talk radio station, an easy listening station, and a country music station. All three made the list of stations I had never listened to but I was interested and jealous all the same.

"I heard you were doing standup comedy." said Jenny.

"Once in a while," I answered.

"Have you ever thought about radio?" she asked.

"I really don't have time to go to school right now." I said, hoping she would buy the excuse.

"You won't need it." She assured me, "With your comedy I bet they would love to have you."

She then told me she would talk to some people and took my phone number. We couldn't talk any longer because someone behind her really wanted a burrito.

A few days later I got a phone call from Jenny asking if I had time to meet with the program director for one of the stations. I traded my apron for a tie and went right in.

The P.D. (our fancy way of saying program director) was also the morning show host of the country station and shared those duties with a female cohort. He immediately asked me about my comedy experience and said they needed some help in their show because no one there was funny.

He offered me a job working overnights and writing for the morning show. All three of the radio stations owned by this company were in the same building and all three went into prerecorded stuff overnight.

All I would have to do is record some weather updates every few hours, make sure the stations remained on the air, and prepare comedy bits for the morning show. I thought it over for about two seconds, kissed his ring, and gave my notice at the taco place.

Working the overnights gave me free rein. I had the entire place to myself from 10 pm to 4:30 am. I had that much time to look through the papers, news wires, and have suitable comedy ready to go by the time the morning show team came in.

Finding hot stuff to talk about was pretty easy. There was always something in the news or a day in history or something to get an idea from. The learning curve was trying to figure out how to produce everything.

I quickly taught myself how to work all the equipment. When I started there we were using CDs and I recorded my bits on reel to reel machines. I learned how to splice tape, mix in sound effects, and worked up a wide variety of character voices. I did things from silly phone calls to full blown production bits with several different voices and sound effects.

The overnight gig went on for about a year until the P.D. informed me they wanted to make a change. I was ready to pack my things but then realized I had no things to pack.

Then the P.D. told me it was he that was doing the packing. He got a job offer in Kansas or some place and was taking his morning show partner with him. He then told me I would be moving to mornings.

I was shocked but ready to make the move. I knew how to do the bits. The only thing I had not done yet was the live stuff but how hard could that be right? (Perhaps this is an appropriate time to remind you I was chronically insecure and pessimistic, making Woody Allen look like Superman.)

I was told I would be getting a morning show partner named Ron Dean. Ron was no stranger in the world of local radio. He had worked in the business for years and mornings were his specialty. I used to listen to him when I was a kid getting ready for school.

He would do comedy bits of his own and he had a gift for impressions. He mimicked them in a creative way adding his own special style to each celebrity. Ron was a true veteran and an extremely talented radio host and that scared the hell out of me.

Unfortunately, I could not see Ron as a blessing but rather a curse. This was not a partner but a competitor. My negative thoughts went to work immediately and I felt this guy was going to push me out before we even got started. After all why would they need me when they had him?

I was told Ron could not start until the next week so I would have to do two morning shows alone. I had just two problems with this. The first being I never done anything on the air live before and the second being I had never listened to country music.

"It's easy" said my already-out-the-door P.D. "All you have to do is play the songs that are printed out on the playlist."

Our CDs came from music companies and were not always the kind you buy in the store with one artist. Some of them had twenty songs with twenty different artists and twenty different formats. You could have Garth Brooks and the B-52's on the same disc. The only thing you had to do was cue the disc to the number that matched the one on the playlist.

This seemed easy enough until my nerves got in the way and I misread one of the numbers. To this day I believe I am the only one to play the heavy metal band Twisted Sister on a country music station.

In a way I think my P.D. did me a favor by

throwing me into the fire like he did. By the end of the first four hour day I had things down and was even doing some live silly phone calls of my own.

In addition to the character calls, I found great joy in the real calls. I soon realized taking calls from listeners was just like talking with audience members when I was doing standup. It gave me the same challenge to ad lib something and more importantly, the same rush.

By the next week when Ron started I was ready to fight comedy fire with comedy fire. I had several comedy bits loaded and ready to go. All he had to do was sit back and let me be the star.

In addition to the morning show, Ron also did afternoons on the AM talk radio station and owned a small advertising company, so we never had time to go over things and establish who was doing what. I knew with his experience he could do whatever he wanted to and I wasn't going to take that lying down.

Within minutes of him coming in the door I hated him. He was nearly 30 years older than me and looked in great shape. He looked like a celebrity and knew what he was doing right from the start.

We had about 30 minutes to make each other's acquaintance and decide what our show would be like. Within seconds I was desperately telling about my standup career and that I had loaded many funny routines into the tape machine.

My panic and desperation must have been quite transparent because Ron treated me with kid gloves for the first few weeks allowing me and even encouraging me to do what I wanted.

After a while I think he caught on to the competitive nature of things and started to bring in recorded bits of his own and for the first three months we never teamed up in the comedy but only played our solo attempts.

I always felt my comedy was more sophisticated than Ron's. He would do things like impersonate presidents and Elvis and carry on conversations with them in both his and their voices. I, on the other hand, created a character called Snots the Clown that would make fart sounds and drop his pants.

Competition in comedy is truly a funny thing. Everyone in the world likes and needs to laugh so you would think the market for humor would be big enough to allow everyone with a sense of it to come in and play.

Ron had been in the business far too long and knew too well that radio was a very competitive business. Entertainment is one of the few jobs where you can come in on time, do whatever is asked of you without complaint and still get fired. Most people who have been in radio for more than a few years have been fired and Ron was not unaccustomed to that rule. Being in the business for over twenty years had gotten him fired more than once.

It was never anything he did. Often times a station will get purchased from some outside company and as a matter of policy they will fire all the main personalities and bring in their own people. Morning show host are usually the first to go.

In radio the mornings are prime time and have

by far the largest number of listeners. The morning show hosts are the poster children of the station. When the station gets bought, they go out with the old station.

I give this rather long explanation of the way radio works in order to allow you to get a glimpse of what was going on in Ron's mind. He had the same fears I did but for more realistic reasons. He had the experiences to back up the paranoia. I just had the paranoia.

Half-way through our first year we were at each other's throats. There were shows where the only time we talked to each other was on the air. Off the air we were bitter enemies, both worried the other was trying to be funnier and take the other's job.

Even though we hated each other, the audience never had a clue and ratings for the station went up. We had more and more fans calling us up every morning. We were often asked to do live appearances and people would ask us for our pictures and autographs. We loathed each other but the listeners loved us.

The interactions with fans eventually saved the show. We soon realized what we were doing was working and no one saw us as individuals but as a team. In radio this is a good thing because no one wants to split up a successful team. We finally felt our jobs were safe and actually began working together.

Once the team began to form we settled into roles that fit our comfort zones. Ron was the veteran and the leader and he became the straight man while I took on a more funny man role. Soon we developed a rhythm and could read each other so well that most of our comedy was ad lib.

We found it worked better if Ron looked through all the wires and news stories and decided alone what we were going to talk about. He was a true pro at knowing what would make good conversation and we both relied on my ad lib skills to make something funny out of it.

But again, the place we really shined was in the phone calls. We took every phone call live and talked with each caller on the air. It would usually begin with Ron asking the caller what they were doing or where they worked and it was my job to turn the conversation into something funny.

Doing ad lib was not only a rush it was also the only time I did not feel insecure. Sometimes I would battle negative thoughts before a show or after but never during. When I was doing comedy I was in a moment of peace that allowed me to just go with my instincts and not worry about anything else. Like in standup, it was the spontaneity that saved me.

The audience ate it up every morning and our live appearances grew very large crowds. We felt like celebrities and it did not take much time for me to abuse that feeling.

TWELVE

Life at home was far from the feeling of celebrity status I had at the radio station. My name continued to be Shit for Brains and the fighting continued to be a daily ritual. The only time we were not fighting was when we were making up and one of those make-up moments led to the greatest blessing of my life.

News that my wife was pregnant gave me hope for our marriage and my future. It fit right in play with the Hallmark lifestyle I had dreamed of and I wanted to make sure I was a better dad than my own.

But as time went on the arguments got even worse. The pressures of pregnancy affected my wife in a very negative way. She became even more emotional and I would often come home to find her crying uncontrollably. On one of those occasions I tried to console her but she began to pound her stomach screaming she did not want the baby inside her.

I was devastated to hear this and my feelings toward my wife continued to change for the worse. A few times during our marriage my wife would see a psychiatrist and told me she had been diagnosed with severe depression. I didn't know what that was and found myself dismissing it as some kind of excuse for bad behavior.

I did not see how depression could lead to such negative thoughts and paranoia toward having a child. I just saw her being difficult and mean. As a result, I began to feel nothing but resentment toward her and began to spend more time at the radio station.

In radio nothing seemed real. It was a fantasy world and I found myself doing things I would never do in the real world. The craziest thing I ever did was ride a live bull. Being a country radio station, we would often sponsor rodeos and that usually meant having some riders on the show with us for a quick interview to plug the event.

During one such interview I got the idea it would be funny to ride a bull on the air. I was always thinking of comedic ideas and very rarely thought of the dangers. So in a true ad lib I asked the riders if they could give me a crash course in riding and two weeks later I found myself in a ring surrounded by cowboy hats and mounting an angry bull.

In order to capture all the excitement for our listeners we had a recorder duct taped to my chest. I borrowed some gloves from a dude, donned my baseball cap from the Second City club in Chicago and was ready to go.

Before I continue I would like to say a few words about cowboys. They are nuts. They have no worries about anything and something like a bull ride is like a walk in the park. One rider who helped to train me by putting me on a barrel and shaking me to death was there to help me get on the real thing for the first time. Without hesitation he spit some chewing tobacco on the back of the bull's neck.

"See that spit?" he said calmly.

"How could I not?" I said shaking like Don Knotts.

"Never take your eyes off that spit." he ordered. "If you look anywhere else, you will fall in that direction."

"You know you could have placed a piece of tape there." I said, knowing we still had some left from taping the recorder to my chest.

Cowboys must prefer spit to tape because he ignored my plea for cleanliness and told me to mount the bull and to squeeze my knees into him as hard as I can. The bull immediately voiced his disapproval of this by leaning into one of the side rails trying to crush my right leg.

"He doesn't like that" I said in defense of the bull.

"He hates all of this," laughed my tobacco spitting friend.

I was forced to agree knowing how much I would hate to be ridden and spit on.

As soon as the cowboy made sure my right hand was secure on the handle thing on the saddle and my left hand was flailing in the air he yelled to them to open the gate and like lightning we were off.

The time to win in a bull ride is just eight seconds and I now understand why. Even five seconds feel like an eternity when you are squeezing a big hairy bull between your thighs and neither of you are enjoying anything about it.

As the time clicked to five seconds I noticed the disgusting chew goober I was to keep my eye on began to slide down the right side of the bull's neck. Being a diligent rule follower, I watched it slide all the way to the ground. (Duct tape would not have done this.)

Just as the cowboy said, I fell directly where my eyes went. Right on top of the disgusting glob of spit up chew. And just to make sure I knew I was not appreciated, the bull rose up his back legs and trounced them onto my right knee. I told him the feeling was mutual and hobbled out of the corral while an ugly clown kept me covered by distracting the bull with an interpretive dance routine.

They checked my knee and told me nothing was broken but I had a large gash to remember my fun time at the rodeo. The cowboy said I should be proud of myself and he was hoping my gash would turn into a scar so I could always remember the event. I told him I would remember it just fine. That night I had nightmares. Not about the bull but rather the spit.

Even the birth of my son became a radio event. My wife's water broke just as I was getting ready to head to the station. I called Ron, slipped on the wet spot, and we drove to the hospital. I tried to remain calm but looked like an out of control bobble head as I tried to keep an eye on the road and my wife at the same time.

My son was eight weeks early and the birth happened within minutes. Soon he was being rushed to the baby intensive care unit and placed in an incubator. The doctor came in and told us all was fine and the baby was doing well. I took that as my cue to call the station and give a live report from the hospital.

For about a week my son, Trevin, remained inside the glass cube and we sat with him every day. We were able to hold him briefly but the isolation left a feeling of sadness and the loss of control made me quite uncomfortable. But I was a dad now and I wanted badly to make things work with my wife.

Even with the emergency birth we got along great at the hospital and were very happy people to have our new addition. Soon we were able to bring Trevin home and for a while it looked as though things were going to be okay but in no time at all we were fighting again and my wife's depression seemed to get worse and worse.

One time I was putting up Christmas decorations and we were arguing about the job I was doing. I was on a chair hanging garland and she came up and slugged me in the back as hard as she could. Looking back I wonder if I could have avoided that by hanging mistletoe instead.

Another time I thought it would be funny to play a prank and poured a cup of cold water on her while she was in the shower. She yelled, "You bastard!" and I thought that was the end of things. After her shower she dried herself off, put on some clothes, came out and slugged me just below the neck.

I have to give her credit. She always seemed to find creative spots to hit me.

I never hit her back but I did do things to hurt her. The celebrity status brought more than people wanting autographs. It also brought women wanting much more. They came out of the woodwork. Sometimes I would get approached at live events, other times they would call to talk to me and some even began showing up at the studio.

At first I didn't know what to do. I had always been far too insecure to ever have been a lady's man but as I said, radio was a fantasy land.

One summer night were doing a live broadcast at a lake for the Fourth of July celebration. We always did live broadcast from a large trailer made up to look like a giant boom box. To listeners it was cool but to Ron and me it was a pain in the butt. We were the ones that had to hitch this to an old truck and lug it all over town. One Saturday the truck stalled on Ron in the middle of an intersection and he vowed never to drive it again so I took the steering wheel from then on, including the Independence Day broadcast.

There was a beautiful woman there that had been to a few of our events and had flirted with me for some time. Being new to the womanizer game I could never tell for sure if a woman was flirting with me or whether they just thought I was funny.

The broadcast ended at midnight and Ron headed home while I shut down the equipment and got things ready to haul back to the studio. As I was putting things away, the woman came in and kissed me. In the good guy movies this would be the part where the hero pushes the girl away and declares the love for his wife and new born son. But I wasn't a good guy. That night in the boom box I officially cheated on my wife.

Afterward she got into her car and drove off and I drove the boom box trailer back to the station. When I got there I realized I had forgotten to bring down a very large broadcasting antenna and bent it like a twig on all the street lights coming back. I'm sure there must have been quite a racket when this rather large and thick antenna hit every street light from the lake to the station but I did not hear a thing.

I was too busy playing back what happened in my mind. I wasn't proud of it. As a matter of fact I hated myself for it. Once again my dream of a Hallmark family was shattering and I had no one to blame but myself.

My wife and son were sound asleep when I got home that night. I crept into my son's room and watched him sleep for hours that night. I also apologized to him for what I did and for what I was about to do.

The next day, I told his mom I wanted a divorce. I could no longer live the way I was and fight every day. I blamed her for everything and refused to even notice that I was being responsible for my own destruction. I even blamed her for having depression and accused her of using it as an excuse to be mean.

And then I told her that I had cheated on her because I could not stand her anymore. Suddenly I was being a total jerk to her and sounding like one of those guys who break up and humiliate their wife on the daytime trash talk shows.

To my wife's credit she wanted to get counseling and try to save the marriage even after my harsh words, but I was already out the door. By the time my son turned one, his parents were no longer living in the same house.

Soon I had an apartment and a lawyer. My lawyer told me there would be no way I could get custody of my son and I should play nice and try to just get as much visitation as I could. Like an idiot, I believed him and did not fight for anything but I was allowed to have my son every weekend and I still tried to be a good dad when he was with me.

When he was gone I continued my downward spiral. I was no longer using drugs or alcohol to feel better about myself. Now I was using women. Anyone that says there is something different about a man that sleeps around as opposed to a woman is a liar. There was no question about it. I became nothing more than a whore.

Nearly every day I was out with someone, either flirting or taking things as far as they could go. During those moments I felt free of all insecurities and negative thoughts but like the drugs, I would crash down hard after the high.

On the days I had my son I was a dad. I never had any dates over and would spend all my time with my boy. We had a ball. Trevin was a very happy child and together we would run around and play and laugh all weekend. But during the week it was back to being a person I did not like.

Radio soon became my existence. I lived and breathed it and cared about little else. My friendships with Jim and the others fell apart and I only spent my time with women.

There was no friendship with any of the women I dated. It was nothing more than a series of one night stands. The next day I would be on to the next one and forgot names more often than I would care to admit. Some of the women were single and some were married. I didn't care and neither did they. It was all about the quick fix -the "feel good"- and then it was over.

It was during this time I came up with a new nick name for myself. I was now calling myself a monster.

As time went on the sex no longer brought me even temporary happiness. The guilt and revulsion I had for myself could not be contained. I began to have mood swings and it got to a point where I could no longer perform sexually. My guilt had overtaken my body and my hatred for myself was now dominating everything I did.

Even my humor was being affected in a negative way. The silly ad lib was replaced once again by the hurtful sarcasm of the monster within me.

I began pushing the envelope further and further and turned our family morning show into a show of controversy. I began to swear on the air and loyal listeners began to turn to other stations. My instinct for humor was gone. Now I was trying to be a mind reader and guess what others thought was funny.

For a comedian to be successful, they have to rely on their instincts. The main thing that makes a comic popular is the simple fact that what the comic thinks is funny also happened to be what others think is funny. When a comic fails to rely on instinct everything falls apart.

Before things could get any worse, the station hired a new general manager and they wiped the staff clean. The Ron and Trev show was over and so were our jobs with that station.

But radio is a funny thing. Across town there was another country station with a P.D. that hated the station I just left. He did not want to hire me for the country station saying it would be like admitting defeat if he hired me from the competition. Instead he wanted me to work for an adult alternative station he oversaw in addition to his country station. Within a week of being fired, I was hired and working again.

THIRTEEN

Ron chose to take a break from radio and focus on his advertising business so I was given a new partner. Actually I was given two new partners. The first one was fired within a few months and replaced with a girl just out of college.

There was a break between the two partners where the P.D. was considering keeping me on the air as a solo because I was doing quite well alone. I found it was not so hard to talk to myself when not taking phone calls from listeners. We also held a contest in which, for one week, I would do each morning's show with a listener drawn from a hat.

For the most part the winners were pretty forgettable and I was getting worn out with people wanting me to be funny off the air as well as on. Previously I would spend our off air time (during songs and commercials) drinking coffee quietly and trying to wake up but when you have a listener with you the entire four hours you find you have to be performing nonstop. By the end of the week I had performed so much I was really annoying myself.

But that Friday brought in something that reenergized me. Her name was Cheryl. A tall gorgeous blonde that made me want to be at the top of my game just to impress her. She ended up being impressed enough to go out with me and soon we were living together.

Cheryl may not have been as impressed with me as she was my son. Trevin and she hit it off right away and we spent most of our time together resembling a family. I even got more visitation time so the three of us could be together more often.

Cheryl was a very athletic person and loved to play sports. She had season tickets to the University of Nebraska football games so we spent every Saturday in the fall watching the Cornhuskers. At that time the team was hot and it was exciting to watch although I did have some trouble with the place we sat.

The view of the game from our seats was great but every Saturday I had to deal with another season ticket holder that sat in front of me. Every game he filled up on stadium nachos and from about half time on I had to breathe in the after effects. One Saturday I got there before him and placed a travel pack of anti-gas tablets on his seat. He never noticed and ended up sitting on them the entire game.

While I was seeing Cheryl I was able to put away my one night stands and say goodbye to that lifestyle. Unfortunately I could not say goodbye to the guilt and continued to struggle off and on in the bedroom. The very act of sex would bring on guilty feelings and I could not separate myself from the monster I felt I was deep inside.

I knew I was a terrible person so why would Cheryl want to be with me? Before long I became paranoid and began to distrust everything she did. If she went out with friends I wanted to know where they went, what they did, and most importantly with whom she did it with.

I became moody and the smallest things would upset me. I put a negative twist on everything Cheryl said. I like to cook and would often make burritos I called "Rook-a-Ritos." Cheryl loved them and told me it was her favorite dish. I then accused her of only liking me for my Mexican food. She thought I was kidding until I left the room in a dramatic huff.

Sometimes I would come home from work and she would mention something I said on the air, saying it was funny. Instead of thanking her I would focus on the stuff she didn't mention and question whether or not she was getting tired of me.

For some reason I was doing whatever I could to destroy the relationship and soon the radio station would lend me a hand. Just like the station before, new management came in and I was fired. Lincoln was not a big town and this time there were no other stations knocking on my door.

Overnight I went from a local celebrity to just some unknown guy. For a few months I was collecting unemployment checks and listeners just don't call you in the morning when you are unemployed. My ego was shattered and my insecurities soared to a new high.

I was sure God had something to do with this and was punishing me for all the bad choices I made in my life. I felt far from loved or forgiven and continued to verify to myself that I was a monster.

After months of searching I finally found a job working at a local television station. I was no longer in the spotlight but behind the scenes as a producer for news programs.

Not being the funny celebrity killed me and I went into a very long pout. I was like a drunk at the end of the bar feeling sorry for himself except I had no drink. I just had the pathetic stories and whininess.

The constant attacks and pouting finally led to Cheryl making the smart choice of leaving me. I often wondered if we would still be together if I hadn't given her the recipe for the Rook-a-Ritos. Now she could make them herself.

I know it broke her heart to say goodbye to Trevin and she would continue to send him birthday cards every year but she was done with me. My moods and behavior were enough for her to not want anything more to do with me and it broke my heart.

FOURTEEN

Working in television is not as exciting as it sounds. The glamour and excitement over the toys you get to play with only lasts about a week before you get the feelings it's just another job.

As a producer I was in charge of two shows, both of them news programs. We didn't have any other local programming. (Sadly, the days of the local shows were gone.) No more kiddy shows or talk shows. We just did the news.

I sometimes wondered why they thought a former comedian would make a good producer of news but I did not want to ask too loud. I was single now and needed the job.

My daily duties consisted of writing news stories, working with news anchors on scripts, organizing the show, and keeping us on time.

Most of the news we covered was local. There were sports, legislature, and city council meetings. I used to have our camera guys get shots of lawmakers sleeping during legislature sessions and we had quite a collection.

Occasionally the national news became the topic of our show as well. I worked some all-nighters during the election standoff between Bush and Gore and I was at the station when the twin towers went down.

I remember walking into work when the first plane hit the tower in New York. Immediately I got together with the newsroom director, the assignment editor, and our lead anchor to plan out our strategy for the rest of the day. As more reports continued to be added to the tragedy, we continued to adjust our plans. When we got word that President Bush was being flown to a bunker in Omaha, we were ready to report it.

We stayed on top of the events and worked side-by-side with the national stations for the next 24 hours. I started to see Dan Rather even when I blinked.

By the next day our news director told us to go home and get a few hours sleep and come back. It was not until I got into my car before I realized what we had just been covering and I sat in the parking lot and wept. I then went home, got some sleep, and went back to the station to continue writing the news.

The fast pace of the news can be stressful and I owe a lot to an anchor by the name of Serese. She was energetic, talented, and jumped in wherever she was needed. When she wasn't writing scripts or editing video footage, she was helping me call reporters to make sure they got their stories in on time.

On her first day we were told to go have lunch

and get to know each other since she would be doing the shows I was producing. In minutes we were laughing and getting along great.

In addition to being a wonderful friend Serese helped me in my spiritual path. She was a Christian and we would have many talks about our faith.

She told me once,

"Christianity is not a private club. All of us are sinners and no one should be left standing outside."

Even while she said this I had trouble believing her. I was still struggled with thoughts toward Jesus. I felt like one of the people standing on the outside. With my broken relationships and all the one night stands, I could not see a loving Christ. I still saw a disappointed Christ looking down and shaking his head.

One morning she came in with two identical books and for about a week she began to read from one of them over lunch. Eventually my curiosity got the best of me while she was reading one of them.

"What are these?" I asked.

"They're daily scripture lessons." She said.

"Why do you have two of them?" I asked

Without looking up she answered,

"The other one is yours if you want it."

"What do you mean it's mine?" I asked.

"Just what I said." She said without mixing words.

"You want me to read it?" I asked.

"Well I don't want you to eat it." She answered.

I grabbed the book and began to look it over. Eventually we began studying the book together and talked each day about the scriptures before getting started on the news.

Each daily lesson was uplifting and I really enjoyed going through them. Serese found a way to start my days on high notes and every evening as I left work she would smile and say, "Have a blessed evening."

For a while I did not know how to reply. No one ever told me to have a blessed day. Often times I would reply sarcastically with a "Please stop drinking at work," but eventually I would just say "You too." I just couldn't say it back. It still didn't seem right for a guy like me to say it with all the baggage I had.

I guess Serese's Christian ways began to rub off on me. It was because of her I started to really pray. I started doing it every night and would say the same thing, "Thank you God for another sober day and please protect myself and my loved ones from any harm or discomfort of any kind. Amen." The discomfort included being protected from mice.

I saw Serese pray before meals and I saw her pray for people. If there was something good going on, big or little, Serese would give credit and thanks to God. When things were not going good she would still give thanks to God for giving her strength.

One morning a reporter came in and started complaining about a news piece Serese wrote. I wasn't surprised because this reporter complained about everything. She was the kind of person that would say things about you under her breath while standing right in front of you.

That morning she was out shooting a story she

was working on and to help her with time, Serese wrote the script for her. When she came in she took one look at it and said, under her breath in front of everyone,

"Whoever wrote this is crap."

To that, five foot Serese stood up tall and said,

"Why don't you…"

And then stopped and sat down in her chair. I was kind of hoping for a brawl but when I looked at Serese she had her eyes closed for a minute and then looked over to me.

"Sometimes praying for people is the hardest thing to do." She said with a smile and I laughed out loud.

Serese's ongoing prayers brought out memories of an aunt I had not thought of for years. Her name was Penny and she was my mother's sister in-law.

She died when I was young and while I do not have many memories of her, the memories I do have are of Penny praising Jesus.

When we ate, she prayed, when we talked she prayed. I even remember we were heading to the store for underwear and before we left, Aunt Penny prayed.

When I was just about 5 or 6, Aunt Penny got cancer and I remember seeing her just before she died. She was in bed and in a lot of pain but never once talked about herself. She only wanted to tell us how much Jesus loved us.

I remember being so shocked to see someone dying and not even being scared. If it were me I'd be screaming like a crazy person but for reasons I couldn't understand, Aunt Penny was filled with happiness.

Serese continued to encourage my steps into spirituality and I yearned to live a normal life. I was even asking girls out for genuine dates. It was strange. In my radio days asking someone out was simple. The one night stands took very little effort to arrange but now I wasn't looking for something shallow.

Now I was trying to be like a regular person. I knew other people would go on dates and just enjoy conversation over a meal or something and then they would go to their own homes for the evening and maybe get together again sometime. I wanted to be a part of that normal life.

A few of the dates I went on came right from the show I was producing. First I asked out a reporter who ordered the most expensive thing on the menu and as she ate, told me she did not find me attractive.

Another date came from one of our interview segments we did each week on medical issues. Our guest was a doctor and after we had dinner she took me on a tour of her office and showed me a funny picture on her wall. I don't remember what the picture was but for some reason I inhaled weird when I laughed and made a terrible squeaking noise. At first I was embarrassed but then I thought, being a doctor, she might be interested in finding out what the squeak was. Apparently she wasn't because she never returned my calls after that.

Another girl I dated for a short while was a sergeant in the army. I took her to a Christmas party being put on by the TV station and we sat with Serese and her date.

I was asked to make some announcements at the party and had left the table for a short time. Later that night Serese assured me this was not the girl for me.

I had no idea what she could have seen in such a short time and then on the ride home my date referred to Serese, who happens to be African American, as "That colored girl." This time it was I that did not return any calls.

FIFTEEN

Sadly, as much of a mentor Serese was, I had to leave the TV station for another job. Being single and having my son several days a week meant I would need to find a way to make more money or we would have to live in a tent somewhere.

Eventually I found a job with a little more pay at a local hospital. (Before anyone has conniptions please note, I was not doing anything medical.)

I worked as a video production specialist. I was hired to make training videos for staff members and would also do promotional videos for the general public.

I am not sure how I got the job, being that I really had not acquired much of a portfolio. I learned the trade on my own while producing the news. I think I may have been hired because the person who interviewed me thought I was Jewish. I don't mean that in a bad way. It's just that after I was hired she asked me what I was doing for Passover.

The job was a simple one. Just make videos for

every department all of the time. The first few days I wondered if I would be doing anything at all. There were no video request and no one was coming to see me. I sat at my desk teaching myself their editing software and watching Jerry Springer on a TV.

At the end of the week, my boss came in and asked me to attend a meeting with her. At last I thought I would see something more to the hospital than my desk and the bathroom. We walked into the meeting room and I was introduced to about twelve nervous looking people all in a hurry to get the meeting underway.

Congress had just passed a privacy bill known as HIPAA. It was a bill that protected patient's rights and was set to be implemented in thirty days. The nervous people I met were the team assigned to educate over 3,500 employees.

They all wanted to know if I could write and produce a video within a few weeks so they would not get in trouble with the Clinton administration. Being new to the job I told them absolutely.

I got the information from one of the team members and wrote the script the same day. I didn't have the heart to tell anyone that I had never made an educational video in my life and did not know what I was doing.

I relied on the only experience I had and wrote it as a comedy. I cast myself in the lead role because I intended to ad lib much of my dialogue. I figured as long as I knew the basics of the law I could make up the rest.

As soon as I got things rolling we had another meeting where I was supposed to give a progress report. I informed them I was making a comedy and saw everyone in the room turn pale. It was then I learned the difference between left-brained and right-brained people.

Left-brained people are very fact oriented. They pay attention to detail and numbers. They are responsible and work hard dotting every "i." Right-brained people, like me, are on the creative side. We are dreamers and lucky we can function enough to drive a car.

A successful hospital runs primarily on left-brained people and we should be thankful of that. After all they are the ones cutting us open and inserting bills. We want to make sure they are focused and not thinking about jokes while resetting a bowel.

When the video was finished we made over 200 copies and sent it out to a number of departments. In one week all employees were required to see the video.

I sheepishly made rounds, snuck into the backs of rooms and listened at the cracks of doors for reaction and it was better than I had hoped. People were laughing in all the right places and even applauded at the end. I couldn't believe someone would actually applaud a mandatory training video.

Within days I was being recognized in hallways and people were telling me how funny I was. Soon I was in demand and everyone wanted me to make a video for them. In a way it felt like radio again but this time I wanted to do things right.

I did not want to go from funny guy to hospital floozy so I tried as best as I could to keep my nose straight. But it didn't take long before I found my nose was still a bit crooked.

Even though people were treating me like a celebrity I was still having the same destructive thoughts and feelings inside. The insecurities were there and I worried I would not be able to continue being funny for long. I was sure people would soon grow tired of me and I would be washed up again.

I always wondered why I never started drinking or using drugs again. I had the same urges for a fix as a drug addict, but for me it was a little different.

For me life was like a rope hanging over a bottomless pit. No matter how hard I hung on, I always knew that eventually my grip would give way and I would fall. That feeling of hopelessness caused me to reach out for assurances no matter how meaningless or short termed they would be.

I began to see a married woman at the hospital. The rendezvous took place in her office and sometimes at my apartment but it did not last long.

I had been getting together with Serese once a month since I left the TV station. We would get together and have Chinese food while updating each other on our lives. During one particular dinner, Serese told me she was now engaged to a wonderful man and was very happy. I didn't tell her what I was doing and went home feeling like a tramp. The next day I broke things off and vowed to get it right this time.

Again I was reminded of the Jesus thing that Serese had and I did not. She just seemed to shine brighter because of it and at times I really resented her for it. But other times I knew I wanted what she had.

I tried praying again and asked Jesus himself to straighten me out but I continued to feel lousy. I was starting to tell myself the praying was a waste of time until one morning when I was getting ready for work.

I heard a voice saying. "It's going to be okay."

I thought I left a TV on or something and checked the house for voices but the voice came through again loud and clear. "Trever, it's going to be okay."

For a minute I was frozen and questioned my sanity.

"Who is this?" I asked out loud feeling stupid.

"You are going to be fine and will tell them about me." The voice answered.

I was sure I was going crazy because in my heart I knew I was hearing the voice of Jesus Christ.

"Why is all this happening?" I asked, not really sure what to say.

"All will be okay, Trever"

And then the voice said something that knocked me down.

"I love you, Trever."

I sat down on the edge of the bathtub with tears streaming down my face and said out loud, "I love you too."

I then realized I was wearing nothing but underwear and wondered if Jesus noticed I had gained some weight. If so, I would blame it on all the Chinese food with Serese.

For the next few days I tried to dismiss what had happened but could not deny what I heard. So rather than deny the voice, I chose to deny the feeling that Jesus wanted me to do something.

I told myself there was no way Jesus would be calling on me. I was still making bad choices in life. I had just had an affair with a married woman, I was still filled with negative thoughts, and I was still a sinful man.

I assured myself that Christ had the wrong person. Maybe he was looking for the tenant who rented the apartment before me. This is why you should always leave a forwarding address. I decided to ignore the experience and never told anyone about it.

While I disregarded the experience, I could not seem to close my eyes to negative thoughts or unhappiness. On one of our Chinese food meetings Serese threw the question out there.

"Have you ever looked into Depression?"

"I'm not depressed." I assured her and she didn't press any further. I wondered why she would ask such a question. I wasn't sad or anything. The feeling I had more often than others was anger. I was angry at the world and held negative views about anything. I didn't trust anyone and always hated myself.

SIXTEEN

Work kept coming in at the hospital and I continued to turn training videos into little comedies. At least once a day someone would stop me in a hallway or elevator just to tell me how funny I was.

When I was in radio this meant a lot because it helped to sustain me, but at the hospital it was no longer working. I continued to be the clown on the outside but on the inside I was losing my grip on that rope.

When one's brain is conditioned to seek quick fixes one turns to the things that have worked in the past. The comedy wasn't helping anymore so I tried to return to normal dating. I continued my search for a hallmark life. I felt, if I could only find a good old fashioned normal relationship, I would find happiness and my troubles would be over. I was always looking for happiness to come from the outside because I could not find it within.

I was working on a training video when a woman came into the department to speak to someone in another office. I worked in a department with trainers for various learning things. I worked there over ten years but to this day I am still not exactly sure what anyone else did in that department.

Whenever I meet someone I turn into the comic and I never learn anything from a conversation. The good part of this is everyone laughs and finds me delightful. The bad part is I walk away not even knowing their name.

As I was saying, a woman walked into the department. When she left I asked who she was and then found some excuse to email her. I acted like I got the wrong person and then started a conversation with her.

Her name was Jackie and she was a director in charge of something or other in the hospital. After about three emails I asked if she would like to have dinner. Two nights later we were having Mexican food and enjoying each other's company. She refused to let me pay for her half saying this was a "get to know each other dinner" and not an official date. At the end of the dinner I asked if I could cook her something at my apartment as an official date and she said yes.

I went all out for the dinner and bought choice steaks and all the kinds of fancy side dishes I could think of. I put on some Mozart to give the impression that I was smart and lit some candles to hide the smell of my son's room.

That night we talked, laughed and really enjoyed each other's company. One of the subjects that came up was religion. It was important to her to know what my religious beliefs were. I told her I was a Christian and then gave the old line of 'I'm spiritual but not religious.' I said this whenever someone asked me if I went to church. The truth was I liked to sleep in and was about as scared of churches as I was of colleges.

She let the comment slide, told me she belonged to a Methodist church, and invited me to come try it sometime. I said "sure" knowing sometime could mean never and made a pot of coffee. We talked most of the night and got along great. Around 2 am I walked her to the door and we kissed each other goodnight.

I spent the rest of the night washing dishes and feeling proud of myself for having a normal date. It was as if I followed the steps I learned from Dick Van Dyke and I wondered if I had found my Laura Petrie.

We began dating about once a week and would email each other in between. After a while we decided to introduce each other to our children. I had Trevin and she had two boys.

The kids got along well but before long I found myself getting irritated by anything anyone did. It seemed the closer everyone became, the less happy I was. Regardless of my growing skepticism I asked Jackie to marry me.

I seemed determined to get that normal family and convinced myself that marriage was the key to my happiness. Besides, Jackie not only made good money and owned her own house, she was intelligent and I enjoyed talking with her.

Within a few months of dating we were in

Colorado getting married. Jackie had always loved the mountains and I had never seen one so we decided bring the kids along and combine our wedding with our first family vacation.

I think both Jackie and I wanted things to work but I am sure she saw some red flags from the beginning. My pessimism was spreading and began to affect every part of my life. I had negative things to say about everyone and everything from work to friends to our family.

The first real negative complaints were regarding our home. I hated that Jackie and her two boys had lived there for so long and felt so comfortable. I told her it always felt as if I was just a guest in someone's house and complained there was no place there for me or my son. I believe my edginess toward the home was actually resulting from my forever growing insecurities which were now being joined by anxiety. I started to worry about everything from people not liking me to the possibility of home invasions or violent attacks.

I closed the blinds all over the house so people could not see in. I became cautious of strangers and would often stare them down with a look of intimidation so they would not even come near. Jackie became quite frustrated with my delusions and mistrust of others.

After a rather uncomfortable first year we tried to ease tensions by purchasing a new home. It was our hope that we would all be able to begin again as a family and share new experiences together but even as we were carrying in the boxes I began staking out territories and soon took over the basement for myself.

I built a studio down there and would continue to feed my creative drive by writing and producing comedy videos. I always loved slapstick and made several comedy shorts involving me basically getting beaten up by various inanimate objects.

On film I played a child-like fool but in life I wasn't child-like. I began to yell at everyone and would often accuse our kids of doing things they didn't do.

We had a rule the boys were to have no friends in the house while the parents were gone. I came home from work early and was sure I would catch someone doing something. Our kids were not malicious but I was mistrusting of the world and everyone in it.

When I came home, Jackie's eldest came out to say hello but I saw someone's arm in his room before he closed his door. Before he could say anything I was yelling and screaming at him and telling him he could never be trusted.

He asked me what I was talking about but I only yelled louder and told him to sit in his room and wait until his mom got home. Then I would show Jackie just how distrustful her children were. Confused, the boy went back in his room and as he opened the door again I realized the arm I saw was a jacket hanging on a chair. After realizing I made a mistake, I reluctantly apologized to him and made a fast retreat to the basement.

In addition to the new home, Jackie continued efforts to suppress my darker side by bringing me to her church. Like she said, it was a Methodist church but it wasn't really in a church. The congregation was just starting out and meeting in a local middle school. Every Sunday they would move chairs into the school's cafeteria/auditorium and set up the small stage with musical instruments.

Although I did have a fear of church people I decided I may need this and went with Jackie. My first visit was a bit nerve-racking. Like I said, church people made me very nervous. Like the college students, these people were above me in many ways. I figured they were obviously happy and not doing the sinful things I was doing. I felt they could see right through me and judged me accordingly. Walking in with Jackie made me feel like I was meeting a room full of fathers that knew I was not good enough to be with their daughter. My palms begin to sweat the moment we sat down in the small cafeteria chairs.

The service began with music and I was surprised how upbeat it was. I could swear I was listening to regular rock and roll with a Jesus twist. Making sure I did not leave my negative thoughts outside I began to judge the lead singer by first attacking the way he was dressed. The guy looked like he just woke up from an all night party and came to church. He was wearing ripped jeans and some t-shirt with faded writing in it. The people there didn't seem to mind as most of them were wearing jeans and casual type shirts as well. I began to wonder how these people were better than me. I knew they were, but just could see why they dressed like I usually did.

After the music a thin well-dressed man came on the stage and placed a little notebook on a music stand that had been left by the band.

In contrast to the rocking music before him, the preacher talked in a very calm and very soothing tone. He talked about some bible verse or Jesus thing but he did it in a way that sounded as if we were all just sitting around having coffee. He was soft and powerful at the same time.

After the service I was looking to make a quick exit but the pastor's welcoming hand blocked me from the door. He introduced himself as Steve Todd. Not Pastor Todd, or Your Majesty Steve. It was just simply Steve Todd. He told me he was glad I was visiting the church and began to ask the usual introductory questions like where I worked and lived. While his inquiries didn't sound invasive, I still kept some guard up and told him only my name, rank and serial number.

My new wife then butted in and mentioned my comedy work and before I knew it I was volunteering to help with sermons and committed to attend a weekly meeting. While I thought any church service could use a bit of humor I resented my wife for volunteering me.

Resentments became a regular feeling in my marriage. It seemed anything and everything was making me angry and nothing would roll off my back. In addition to the growing anger I also had an increasing need for self destruction. The closer my life came to normalcy the more I wanted to be sinful and destroy things. It was as if I felt I would not survive if I wasn't doing something to cause harm to the world I was living in. I had given up smoking, drugs, alcohol, but there was still something out there I could not gain control of.

For instance, there was a lovely woman who

worked at the hospital. She was only in her twenties; a good ten years younger than me and I dove in to see if I still had it. We made out in closets and in my office after hours. There was nothing more to it than the feeling of knowing we were doing something wrong.

Often times I would end the work day with her in my arms and then go home to eat dinner with my family. My wife never once became suspicious and I was able to hide the affair well from everyone except myself.

I don't know if it was maturity, guilt or just fear of getting caught, but I could no longer sneak around. After just a few months I ended things with the twenty-something. I thought she would be heartbroken but soon found out I wasn't the only man she was meeting in closets. Maybe I didn't really have it after all.

My actions were serving their purpose by continuing to bring my self-worth down to nothing and prove I was a monster. On the surface I would be the happy performing clown delighting people at church and work but at home and in my mind, I was a beast growling at the night and mutilating my existence.

Insomnia became the norm as I would sit up nights wondering what was wrong and wonder why I was so angry and destructive all the time. I also began to lose weight. A blood test showed I was full of triglycerides and cholesterol because when I did eat it was usually crap from some vending machine. I stopped eating with the family because I was too angry and felt too ashamed to join them at the table.

No one ever saw any signs of shame from me. They only saw the anger which by the second year of marriage could be better described as rage. Yelling and punching walls became a daily occurrence at home even as my comedy continued to shine at the church.

To the people at church I was the celebrity who livened up services but to my family at home I was more than they could handle. After about two years of turmoil my second wife filed for divorce. She even paid for the lawyers and agreed to pay off our debts. All I had to do was get out of the house as soon as possible.

SEVENTEEN

While I continued to damage the lives of nearly every person I met, I worked very hard to be the best father to my son. I tried to hide my sins and be more of a dad to Trevin than my dad was to me.

I became one of the Scout leaders to his troop and went to all the meetings. The only trouble with things like this was the fact I never knew what I was doing. I knew very little about scouting. I tried to join the scouts when I was younger but was asked to leave after I taught my troop how to smoke cigarettes.

I never really camped or fished but I tried my best to be a leader and a role model for my son. The big event that summer was a two day camping trip with several other troops throughout the state. My son was more than excited and I went out and bought all the stuff. We had the sleeping bags, the tent, and even some fancy lanterns and flashlights. I bought all the toys a camper would want.

We piled everything into my Jeep and the two of us were off. The drive to the campground was only supposed to take an hour so I began to wonder when I saw we had been on the road for three.

I never was very good at reading maps. When I was in second grade I was diagnosed with dyslexia but never did any research to see what the symptoms were. I'm still wondering if not being able to read a map is one of them.

We stopped for lunch in a small café in Kansas as I tried to figure out why we were no longer in Nebraska. I was also curious as to why we were going south when the campsite was supposed to be to the north.

To my surprise and delight, Trevin grabbed the map from me and began to read it like a true explorer. He found where we were and told us were we needed to go. I gave the map to him and we found the campground two hours later.

A half hour after that we found the troop I was supposed to be leading and set up our tent. I hurt my back falling out of a dead tree while trying to get wood and we built a nice fire.

I thought we could eat like the cowboys and brought a can of baked beans. It wasn't until I put them in a pan before I realized I never bought any silverware. After looking around I decided to stir the beans with stick and made some spoons by breaking a pair of sunglasses in half.

That night we gathered all of our trash and put it in some trash bags. I also brought some bags for all of our dirty clothes. After two days of hiking, fishing and other scout-like things we headed home with Trevin reading the map.

After we got home and began to unpack our gear I realized I had thrown all of our clothes away with the trash from our campsite. Trevin laughed while I got on the phone to order him another uniform and a merit badge for being a good camper.

I always hoped, in addition to the funny stuff, my son would know me as a loving and caring person in his life. Sadly as much as I tried to be a good father, I know my darker side was not so easy to hide.

One night while I was fighting with my wife I stormed down to the basement and started punching the walls and slamming doors. I then remembered being a child and hearing my dad beat the hell out of those metal lockers we had in the basement.

I knew no matter how hard I tried to deny it, in many ways; I was being just like my dad. It was then I felt a bizarre connection to the man I always feared

EIGHTEEN

As my personal life continued to head straight to hell, there was surprising growth in my friendship with Pastor Steve Todd. We started meeting for coffee and lunch often and would talk at first about comedy but eventually the conversations became more serious.

I told Steve about my growing insecurities and struggles with anxiety but I never talked about my rage or cheating. I never spoke of the other personality traits that had labeled me a monster. I still felt too ashamed to share those details with anyone.

As much as I kept from Steve he still seemed able to read me and at times I wondered if he somehow knew of my wrongdoings. If he did know he did not seem troubled by them but rather concerned about my well being.

There were times he told me I was a great leader and was meant for more. He felt God had plans for me even if I could not see them. Like Serese, I felt

Steve saw beyond the crap I was knee deep in and focused more on the person underneath. At times, that really scared the hell out of me.

During one of our conversations, Steve told me he thought I would make a good pastor. I sarcastically told him he would make a good politician. In truth I did not know what to say to that. I doubted his observation and to be honest his words filled me with anger.

I became terrified at the thought of serving God and knew deep down inside I would never be able to shake the dark side within me. As much as I wanted what people like Steve had, I knew I would never come close. After the conversation I told Steve I needed a break from the church. I made an excuse being busy at work and needing some time off but I just needed to get away.

Steve kept calling while I was gone from the church and often invited me for coffee. Sometimes he would say they just needed a little comedy routine for an upcoming Sunday and wanted to know if I could help. I knew he really didn't need the comedy. I knew he was really just concerned.

Steve's persistence eventually won out and I returned to the church to do more comedy bits but Steve had some other plans. He told me he going on vacation and asked me to deliver a Sunday sermon.

I wanted to run again but something was going on inside of me. At first I thought I was just too tired to fight with the politician but there was more to it. Deep down inside of me was a desire to do it. No matter what I did on the outside, there was still a part of me that longed for innocence. I missed the church while being away. I also continued to wonder what it was that church people had that I did not.

Besides, there was something about Steve I trusted and I felt he really did believe in me even if I didn't. I wrote the some notes and looked up some bible passages from the daily reader I shared with Serese.

In a somewhat hypocritical move, I preached on forgiveness of sins. Even as I wrote things about forgiveness, I never felt I was a part of the select group of people Jesus wanted for his kingdom. I always knew I was on the outside looking in. They were the chosen and I was their Judas.

Every time I did something for the church I felt as if I was betraying people. While I was up at the altar telling them all about the love of Jesus, I felt no love inside me. As I talked about living a Christian life I was cheating on people and disrupting lives.

I was a phony but I may have been the only one who knew it. My innocent act impressed the church planning team so much they asked me to create a video series aimed at healthy marriages. After two failed attempts, I knew I could at least write about unhealthy marriages. I thought I could show a healthy marriage if I wrote the opposite of anything I ever did.

While I was filming I met wife number three. She was married at the time with three kids and from the first time I saw her I was felt knocked over. I had never been so attracted to anyone that quickly. In a page from a soap opera horror movie, she was cast in this video series as my wife.

I spent a lot of time talking with her between

filming and really seemed to warm up to her. I kept telling her how good of an actor she was and then started to tell her how good of a person she was. I was so smitten by her I wanted to sweep her off her feet but she had a husband.

I started to ask her questions about her family and noticed a little hesitation when I mentioned her marriage. I took it as a hopeful sign and dug a little deeper.

Eventually she confided in me that she was not happy in her marriage and wanted out. Naturally I put on my best cape and attempted to be the hero that would save her from the awful man she had married. In truth I knew nothing about the man and was only trying to get what I wanted. She would seek advice from me and I would tell her what we both wanted to hear. I was a terrible person to help with any marriage.

Before long we were talking on the phone every night like two teenagers and within months she was filing for divorce. As soon as the divorce was legal we were married. I had many friends tell me it was just too soon but I felt this was the right one for me and it would work this time. After all, she took my breath away every time I looked at her.

It wasn't long before her beauty stirred up my insecurities and soon I was jealous of anyone looking at her. One time a neighbor came to her place to tell her she had a broken sprinkler. As soon as he left I asked her if she had ever had a thing for him.

I became paranoid and mistrusted her friends. There was no way I was going to believe this beautiful woman really wanted to be with me.

Even though she left her husband I was jealous of him too. He was a real manly man and worked on cars, hunted and was built like a brick. I had never been good with cars, I never hunted, and I could barely even lift a brick. In comparison, I just couldn't figure out why I was chosen over him. Also when I saw him, I wondered if that was what my father wanted me to be.

Not only was the macho life something my new wife was used to, it was also what her kids had grown up with. They all hunted, fished, and listened to country music while chewing deer jerky. I could never get myself to try deer, feeling I was somehow going against Santa.

I did try to win them over by going on a turkey hunt. I brought my son and my wife's oldest boy out to some wooded area in the country. We sat for hours in the snow. I had bought some camouflage clothes but was wondering how much they blended in with the white snow. "Maybe if I pretended to be a bush," I thought to myself but then wondered how I would do that.

Trevin and I brought no guns to the hunt. We were just there to see what it was all about. We had shot at some targets in scouts but neither of us really had any urge to shoot at something living.

We both sat there and froze while the hunter was rubbing two sticks together and trying to sound like a turkey. Up to that point I had no idea what a turkey sounded like.

The imitation worked. After several hours of looking at snow we saw about five horny turkeys, thinking two sticks were their mate. We all sat very still and did not move. I held my breath. I was there to win this new family over and did not want to mess anything up.

I only began to worry when I realized I was sitting right between the turkeys and the hunter. I really started to pray the eldest boy liked me enough to wait until I was clear before firing. Thankfully he had a hunter's patience and shot just as a turkey passed beside me. The shot was so loud I fell over the same time the turkey did.

As the rest of the turkeys ran off sounding like a herd of sticks being rubbed together, the hunter went over and stomped on the shot turkey's neck to make sure it was dead. I tried my best not to look shaken up by all of this but inside I wanted to curl up in a ball.

No matter how much I tried to be the macho guy their dad was, I just couldn't pull it off. I wasn't a hunter. I was a clown and clowns use rubber chickens, not shot to death turkeys.

After we got home the eldest son took the dead turkey into the garage and took a sharp knife to remove the feathers. I couldn't watch and went inside. I tried to muster up some courage and went back a bit later only to see him remove the insides of the turkey. I smiled at him. And then casually went inside the house to throw up. Now I remember why I flunked biology in high school.

My darkness increased as did my insecurities and I became controlling in an effort to stay on level ground. I tried to tell my wife what to do and where to go. When she argued with me I would act out and throw things.

I was driving the car when one of our fights broke out and went into an awful rage. I put the gas pedal to the floor and would not let up as we flew through side streets and then into traffic. My wife was terrified and screaming but at that moment I didn't care if we died or killed someone. The worst part about that ride was we were on our way to church at the time.

While I continued to act like a monster, deep down I still wanted to fight it and felt trapped inside this dark place. I still wanted to be free of the anger and negative thoughts but did not know how to escape.

Eventually the physical toll of my emotions brought me to the hospital with an ulcer. At the time the doctors thought I might have cancer and were running some tests and my wife came in to comfort me.

But even my fear of cancer turned into rage. The darker my thoughts became, the more I saw everyone as an enemy. I began to feel as if I was always backed into a corner and the only way I could protect myself was to lash out at anyone around me.

As my wife sat beside me I told her to fuck off and I didn't want her there. Even though I had been so cruel for so long, I still saw an instant look of hurt and shock in my wife's eyes.

When I returned from the hospital I tried desperately to change my attitude. I did an old therapy trick of writing a letter to all the people I thought had done me wrong in life as a way of dealing with my anger.

I wrote to my father and mother. I wrote to drug addicts and friends from the past. I wrote to anyone I thought had crossed me.

I wrote about my dad's anger and about my mom's failure to protect me. I wrote to bullies from childhood. I even wrote to my grandma, telling her I was angry she left me so soon.

I thought if I wrote about my anger in every situation I could finally say goodbye to it once and for all. After I wrote the letters, I placed the letters on a gas grill and lit them all on fire. It was a ceremonial burning symbolizing my rage leaving me and literally being consumed in flames.

For a while my little bonfire seemed to work. I had fewer outbursts and no longer asked my wife a series of investigative questions when she got home from work. I smiled more and became friendlier to others. The only thing that suffered was my comedy.

My creativity became a challenge and I found it more and more difficult to be funny. I began to wonder if my imagination had gone up in smoke with my letters.

Soon I was writing scripts which were much darker and full of cruel sarcasm. I even created a draft for a new series in which I would be playing a very negative and bitter person. I told people it was a parody of the person I used to be but in truth, it was the person I still was.

Soon I realized I had not changed at all but rather had been suppressing my thoughts and feelings in order to hang on to my wife. I was still as insecure and jealous as before but I was holding my thoughts and accusations inside.

I could hold not them for long and soon I was asking the same untrusting questions and accusing her again of not loving me. I made up my mind it was just a matter of time before she left me so I began to sabotage the marriage in an effort to protect myself.

The end came while I was doing a play in downtown Lincoln. I had been asked to be in it and reluctantly accepted the invitation.

I always hated memorizing lines and preferred ad lib but felt it may help my insecurities if I faced some fears in front of a live audience. The play wasn't bad but wasn't great and rehearsals were long and tiring. I hated the time commitment and looked forward to the end of the play's run.

I played a comedic plumber working on the pipes of a famous singer. All of my scenes were with this twenty something and we had to rehearse a lot together. I had already told myself I was going to behave and not fall into the sins of my past.

I still longed for a good marriage and a more simple life but circumstances would again lean toward chaos and soon I was flirting with the young actress. I convinced myself that flirting was okay as long as it did not go any further.

The flirting went from silly talk during rehearsals to emails filled with innuendos. The innuendos must have been easy to read because my third wife filed for divorce soon after reading one of them off my computer.

There was a certain irony in the fact that I had been a cheat for so many years and the one time I got caught was when nothing physical happened at all. But it doesn't take a physical act to betray someone's trust. And the email was not the only reason she was leaving. A week later I was moving into the same apartment I lived in after the divorce of wife number two.

One would think I would have been used to the feelings of divorce but I think there is something to the old saying of three strikes and you're out. With each divorce I felt more lost and heartbroken.

I no longer thought of myself as a monster but more as a demon. For so long I did such harmful things and never wanted to. I was out of control and out of ideas.

While the divorce was underway I remained locked in a contract and still doing performances for the play downtown. It was hell trying to play a funny character while, at the same time, feeling life was not worth living anymore. As I left the house for the theatre one night I grabbed a bottle of sleeping pills.

While I cannot speak for suicidal people everywhere, I can say my commitment to taking my life was not sought out as something dramatically planned. It was more a moment in time where I felt I had in some ways already left my life.

It's difficult to explain but I became numb of all emotions as I drove to the theatre. Why I drove there I really don't know. For some reason my body continued to go through the routines of the day but my mind was already finished. I remember telling myself suicide was the only way I could stop hurting people.

I don't know if it was all the stuff I had been doing with the church but I started to think about Judas in the bible. The whole time I drove I compared myself to him and wonder if this was how he felt after turning Jesus into the authorities. The Bible makes no mention of his thoughts or actions while Jesus was being taken away. It only says he took his life afterward.

When I pulled into the parking lot I knew what I was going to do. I grabbed the bottle of pills and began to think of all the people I had betrayed.

I thought about each one of the women I had slept with and never saw again. I thought about the friends I had isolated myself from. I thought about my wives and the ways I ruined each marriage. I thought of my son and ways I failed as a father. I then thought of God and the many times I refused to listen.

As I pressed down and cursed the child proof bottle I spoke to God one last time. It wasn't a last ditch prayer asking for help and salvation but rather just an apology. I just told him I was sorry. When I lifted my head I was startled to see my friend Jamie pounding on my car door window.

Perhaps the oddest thing about that night was after Jamie took the pills from me and we had our talk, I went into the theatre and did the play. I have no memory of it and don't know how I managed to even say the lines but apparently I went through the motions and no one knew anything had happened.

Jamie attended the play and would not allow me to leave his sight. He also called Steve Todd and for a week I was on suicide watch with each of them taking a day and evening to spend with me. At least the good part of that was I was being taken out to dinner nearly every night. For the record nothing helps a suicide watch more than nachos.

During our conversations, both Steve and Jamie brought up the subject of Jesus and allowing him to help me through things. They both said, "Christ would forgive me for the choices I made in my life," but I couldn't think about anything with faith. I wasn't ready to allow myself to heal.

I had far too good of memory and knew all the things I did in life. I wanted to take the punishment.

I kept thinking about Judas. I also felt I had betrayed everyone around me including Jesus himself. There were many times in life where he reached out to me and each time I turned my back and continued to do things my way.

I lied to Jesus more times than I could remember. Each time I sinned I was fully aware of my actions. Each time I knew I was going against "The will of God."

Like Judas, I put on a Christian show, but inside I was a Devil.

NINETEEN

The suicide watch began to get tedious and soon I was missing my freedom. To ease some of the worry of my bodyguards I promised to seek professional help.

I had been to counseling in the past on several different occasions but it only helps when you tell the truth and I never did that. I got very good at playing the therapy game and telling them what they wanted to hear.

At times I could even get the therapists to open up about their own problems. I remember one occasion the sessions quickly switched focus and I found myself listing to the therapist talk about their marriage woes.

Before I made my appointment to see the shrink I had some coffee with my mother. She knew there were problems and had been told about my suicide attempt. I guess you know it's serious when your friends tell your mother on you.

For the past year my mom had been researching her blood line. My mom was adopted at the age of two and after her adopted mother passed away she felt a need to connect with her biological parents.

Surprisingly, she was able to find some new information very quickly. For one she learned we were of Jewish heritage. I guess that explains why my old boss assumed I was. Mom also learned her mother had died of heart problems which is an issue on my father's side of the family as well.

The most pertinent information she had for me at the time however was a history of mental illness. It seems many of my relatives enjoyed some stays in the institutional communities.

To add a bit of mystery, there was no additional information like, what were they diagnosed with? Were they dangerous? Did they dress up as Napoleon or Hitler?

I thought any tidbit of information would have helped because at this point I felt as if I needed to be behind padded walls myself.

The next day I had my appointment with the therapist and told the truth about everything knowing full well I may be institutionalized like my dear old ancestors.

The therapist had me take a test with multiple choice answers. The questions ranged from "I would like to be a florist," to "I often feel like harming people with sticks." It was somewhat difficult to be honest and not give sarcastic answers. I did that once during an employee placement test in high school and the results said I would make a good chicken boner.

After I took the test the therapist had me wait in a room while my answers were looked over with a fine tooth comb. About thirty minutes later she came in and pulled up a chair in front of me. I always thought it was bad when any kind of doctor or therapist pulls up a chair in front of you. It seems they only do that to deliver bad news or to discuss your bill. Either way the news is usually devastating.

She then told me I was suffering from major depression. I kind of smiled defensively when she used the word suffer. I always thought of depression as sadness and though I felt sad from time to time I had to ask her straight out.

"So other than sadness I am just an asshole?"

"No." she assured me, "there is much more to it than that."

She told me about depression as being something chemical in the body. Neurotransmitters — chemicals that brain cells use to communicate — are out of balance in depression. She compared it to diabetes by saying it was something that affects a wide variety of people and can be treated with medication. Many times the causes can be genetic. As soon as she said genetic I thought about my father. All his life he did not seem happy.

Just a few days after I was put on my new meds, my dad passed away. They said his body had just shut down and there was nothing they could do.

The night he died I was able to kiss him on the forehead and tell him I was proud to be his son. I told him I loved him and he died a few hours later.

The next morning there was a look of peace on my dad's face as if he had finally been relieved of the weight he carried for so many years. I believe my dad finally found happiness the night he passed away.

For the next several weeks I thought about my dad. I also thought about heaven and salvation. I prayed and asked God to take good care of my dad but there were night's I often worried about him.

While I know my dad believed in God, he didn't go to church much or do the many things that are judged as pious by other Christians.

During one prayer I pleaded with God to just tell me my dad was in a good place and that he was happy now. I heard no answer and my worry continued until a week later when I was at a grocery store picking up a box of cereal. As I reached for the box there was a loud and clear voice saying, "Trever, your dad is okay."

It was the same voice that had visited me years before. I knew who it was and I just said "Thank you."

I then brought home the box of Cheerios and ate them straight out of the box the way my dad did when we watched Saturday morning cartoons.

TWENTY

The first thing I noticed about being on antidepressants was I quickly gained 20 pounds. I guess the pills are aimed at getting me to be the jolly fat man I had always hoped to be. It also makes me wonder if Santa Claus ever suffered from depression.

Actually the weight didn't concern me too much because I was feeling better. I don't know what was in those fat pills but I no longer had the anxiety or negative thoughts. I no longer had urges for quick fixes or one night stands.

I wasn't soaring high above the clouds but I was out of the pit and on even ground. For the first time in my life I felt normal, or at least how I thought normal people felt.

I no longer got angry at everything and I was amazed how things could roll off my back. For example, if I went into a store, I used to try to read people's personalities in my mind and always thought negative things about them. I would look at strangers and think they had a grudge against me. Now that I was on the meds, I looked at people differently. I could now see the good in people at the store. I even found myself smiling at strangers.

For the first time in years I felt genuinely happy. I was okay with who I was and where I was. I asked my doctor if my new feeling were normal.

"Think of it like diabetes." She answered. "If a diabetic is unaware they have a chemical imbalance inside them, they will never know why they have dangerous reactions and low blood sugars. They will always feel they are not normal and be at risk of serious problems."

I grabbed a lollypop from her children's bin as she explained more.

"Once a diabetic gets on the correct medication they will begin to feel normal and much better, just like you are taking meds for your chemical imbalance."

As I was leaving her office she said one more thing.

"Always remember, it is not the diabetic's fault for being diabetic and it is not your fault for having depression."

I thank her and left hoping I could believe that.

For the next several weeks I studied up on the symptoms of depression and learned, in most cases, woman and men react differently. While women tend more to feel sadness, men feel more anger and rage. Men also mistrust others and often choose dangerous patterns of behavior like driving fast, using drugs or alcohol, and even cheating and having one night stands.

The more I read the more I saw it in my father

and even in my mother. For years when I was a child she would put on a happy face, but I always saw sadness inside her. I began to wonder if depression was the illness that was evident in my mom's biological family.

After reading all of this and feeling so relieved, I cried out "I'm not an asshole anymore!" for the entire world to hear.

My celebration came to a halt one Friday afternoon when I got the mail. There was a typed out letter with no return address. It began with an edited passage from the Bible. *"The fear of the Lord that is wisdom. Job 28:28"* and then it continued, *"Ambition is that grit in the soul that creates disenchantment with the ordinary and puts the dare into dreams. But left unchecked it becomes an insatiable addiction to power and prestige; a roaring hunger for achievement that devours people as a lion devours an animal, leaving behind only the skeletal remains of relationships."* In place of a signature was one last sentence; *"God won't tolerate it."*

I read the note several times. I was pretty sure it came from my ex-wife or a member of her family, but the source was of little concern. The message itself hit me very hard. It was saying what I knew to be true.

I had hurt so many people in my life for my own selfish ambitions. Whether it was for a quick fix or out of paranoid thoughts, I had betrayed more people than I could honestly remember and the ripple effects were still rolling.

Reading the note, I was again thinking about Judas. The man was called a betrayer because he stepped on others for selfish ambitions. The Bible never gave any excuses for Judas. It never said, "But afterwards, Judas was put on medication and things seemed to work out fine."

I did not feel like an ass anymore. But my actions caused more pain and destruction than I could fathom.

I lied, cheated, stole, bullied, and used people for my own satisfaction. I stepped on others to feel better about myself. I broke up friendships and marriages. No matter what therapy I was in today, I knew I would never be in a place I could justify the sins of my past and no matter how much I had changed, I knew there were people in this world who would always see me as a monster.

After reading the note I sat on the floor of my apartment and cried. I knew there was no way I could erase over 40 years of such sinful behavior and there was no amends I could possibly make to reverse things. No matter what I did from here on, the monster would still be a part of me.

I had given sermons on forgiveness and salvation but could not see in my heart how I could be a receiver of that gift when waves of my transgressions were still rolling through the world.

Around 3 am I grabbed a Bible and began reading about Judas the betrayer.

The other 11 disciples were totally unaware of Judas' plan to turn Jesus over to the authorities. No one knew he was a dishonest man, living a double life.

I was dishonest and lead a double life. I put three wives through hell by yelling, cheating and lying. When a spouse cheats on a spouse, do they not betray with a kiss?

I realize Judas did all these things to Jesus while I did it to everyday people but somehow I saw my actions as the worse of the two. After all, I was stepping on "God's children."

The Bible says Jesus knew what was happening the night when Judas came in with the guards. Did Jesus forgive Judas?

I continued reading the bible looking for answers and found a passage in Mark were Jesus was at the table with his disciples and said one of them would betray him.

"It is one of the Twelve," he replied, "one who dips bread into the bowl with me. The Son of Man will go just as it is written about him. But woe to that man who betrays the Son of Man! It would be better for him if he had not been born."

This little passage did not do much to ease my mind but then I read on and saw, following the acknowledgement of the betrayer, Jesus shared bread and wine with the twelve disciples saying it was his body and blood to fulfill a new covenant of forgiveness of sins.

I had to read it twice along with the versions from the other Gospels before realizing something I hadn't noticed before.

Jesus shared the bread and wine while Judas was still at the table. Was this significant? Did it mean Jesus had forgiven Judas for what he was about to do?

The Bible also says the devil entered Judas. Could it be, that when Jesus was saying it would be better for Judas not to have been born, he was referring to the emotional suffering he would endure having Satan overtake him? I wondered if

Judas killed himself to escape the guilt. I also wondered if that was why I tried to kill myself.

The next morning I wrote letters to my ex-wives telling them how sorry I was. I would have called but many of them did not want anything to do with me. They are all fans of caller I.D.

After I wrote the letters I thought about them not wanting contact and immediately felt the letters were another selfish act and would probably not do much to help them at all. It was again just a way for me to try to feel better about myself.

I was out of ideas and continued to feel miserable about my sins and the harm I caused. In a moment of either helplessness or exhaustion, I laid face down on the floor and prayed.

At first I said nothing at all and just listened to the silence. Then there was only one thing I could say and repeat, over and over again, the same two words. "I surrender."

I also continued to read the Bible each day. I began to read about Paul the apostle who hunted down Christians before becoming one and I wondered if he ever got over the bad feelings caused by his sins. But the more I read about Paul, the more I realized it didn't matter.

And then, like a sucker punch, it hit me. Every person with a mind and soul feels remorse for things done wrong but it's the forgiveness from Christ that makes us change.

There were no actions I could take to right my wrongs because my wrongs would never be right. My sins were, are, and will always be sins. It is only in Jesus Christ that I can be forgiven. And only in Jesus Christ that I can begin again and truly amend my ways.

Like a burning bush to the head I finally got it. I knew my actions were forgiven and by completely surrendering I was finally free to move forward and be a flawed but better person.

Like Judas and Paul I betrayed Jesus and everyone I knew. But, while I chose the path of Judas, Jesus was giving me the path of Paul.

I would like to think Jesus did forgive Judas. I know how bad Judas felt for what he did. Judas did a monstrous thing. I can relate. But if I can be more understanding of Judas, maybe I can be more understanding of myself.

TWENTY ONE

Time passed since I tried my suicide. The play I was doing was long over and my son and I were settled in and enjoying our apartment.

My new pills were keeping me fat and on solid ground while I was learning to do things differently. I returned to the church but this time as a member and not a performer.

While I still love comedy and being funny, I no longer felt I had to do it in order to survive. I was happier to worship God than to perform.

Things were different but I was not a different person. I think, in some ways, I returned to the child playing his room. Painful experiences had aged me but in many ways, they had left me some wisdom. Medication brought me to solid ground, but I think it was Surrendering to Jesus that brought me out of the darkness.

My heart was much more open and I was much happier to be in my own skin. I knew I would always be a sinner but I knew Jesus would always be there with his hand on my shoulder. I really used to be blind and now I finally saw.

Every day I continued to assert my servant hood to Jesus and one afternoon He called me on it.

I was sitting at work when an all too familiar voice returned with just two words.

"It's time."

My mind was immediately filled with all I needed to know about those two words.

I knew I, a sinner, could never judge another person.

I knew what it is like to be shunned and to shun.

I knew what it is like to blame and be blamed.

I knew what it is like to be a monster.

I knew what it was like to judge and be judged.

I knew what it is like to sin.

I knew what it is like to forgive.

I knew what it is like to betray.

I knew what it is like to repent.

I knew what it is like to surrender.

I knew what it is like to be reborn.

I knew how it feels to experience God's Forgiveness.

And I knew at that moment what my entire life had been for. I got on the computer and emailed Steve. I told him I wanted his job. His response was quick.

"You what?"

"How do you become a pastor?" I replied.

"Who wants to know?" he responded sarcastically.

"Remember when you told me I would make a good pastor?" I asked.

"I did?" he replied.

This short conversation continued for several more emails and then carried over into many conversations and meals shared. Steve educated me about the ways of the clergy and told me how to go about becoming a Methodist pastor.

I had new energy and was excited to get started. I also noticed a brain I either did not know I had or was too insecure to look for. I no longer feared colleges and was eager to learn everything I could. The Bible became my permanent companion and for the first time I understood what I was reading.

Telling people about my career move was interesting. There was everything from encouragement to disbelief. I remember telling my son about it.

"Don't you have to go to school for that?" he asked.

"Yes." I answered.

"It's not like when you went to high school," he warned me, "they use things called computers now."

With that sarcastic response and the smile that came with it, I knew I had his blessing. Since then we have had many talks about faith and he has been a huge support. He helped around the house while I worked and learned how to be a clergy guy.

As I write this, it has been a week since I gave my very first Easter sermon. I have been serving as pastor at a church in Tecumseh, Nebraska before I move to my next appointment. Attendance has been great and the people could not be nicer.

As I gave my sermon on the grace of Jesus Christ, I could not help but think of the living proof I am. I was such a sinner and now here I was preaching the "Good News."

During this Easter sermon, I shared communion.

As I broke the bread, I told everyone that they were invited. I told them how Jesus doesn't turn people away. I also told them how Judas sat at the table when Jesus broke the bread. And I told them I knew what it was like to be in that seat.

ABOUT THE AUTHOR

Trever Rook is currently serving as a pastor, and lives a quiet life in Nebraska. At this time, Trever is working on his second book.

29804361R00094

Made in the USA
Middletown, DE
28 December 2018